Legends & Lore
OF
Fort Lauderdale's
New River

To Dori Lynn—

So pleased to meet you.

Good reading.

Don R. Lyn

3/23/2022

LEGENDS & LORE
OF
FORT LAUDERDALE'S
NEW RIVER

DONN R. COLEE JR.

THE
History
PRESS

Published by The History Press
Charleston, SC
www.historypress.com

Front cover. Top left: Frank Stranahan's trading post on New River, circa 1896. *Courtesy of History Fort Lauderdale. Top center*: Tequesta brave harvesting "Bounty from the Sea." *Painting by Theodore Morris, from www.floridalosttribes.com. Top right*: Captain and crew of the *Okeechobee* cruising on a newly dredged Everglades canal. *Courtesy of History Fort Lauderdale. Bottom*: Pristine New River, circa 1884. *Courtesy of History Fort Lauderdale.*

Back cover. Lauderdale Marine Center, located on New River's south fork, is said to be the largest yacht repair facility and shipyard in the United States. *Courtesy of Christopher Savage, Savage Global Marketing. Inset*: Miss Ivy Julie Cromartie, the new town of Fort Lauderdale's first schoolteacher, being courted on New River by Frank Stranahan. *Photograph by Frank Stranahan, courtesy of History Fort Lauderdale.*

First published 2021

Manufactured in the United States

ISBN 9781467148221

Library of Congress Control Number: 2020945777

To Martha MacInnes Colee, my wife, my navigator, my best friend.

CONTENTS

PREFACE

There is nothing "new" about southeast Florida's New River. It was there long before the dredges of the massive scheme to "reclaim" the Everglades for agriculture and development started digging in 1906. It was there before Henry Flagler's railroad steamed south through the newly platted town of Fort Lauderdale in 1896 and before boats navigated the length of Florida's east coast on an inland waterway in 1895. New River was there in 1893, when weary and jostled southbound stagecoach passengers camped overnight on its banks before boarding a hand-pulled ferry to cross its rushing waters while en route to today's Miami. New River was there before the American flag flew over the new state of Florida in 1845 and before it became a U.S. territory in 1822. Seminole Indians plied New River's waters and banks for food after they fled south, chased by General Andrew Jackson in the first of three wars against their people in 1817.

The first white settlers were documented along the New River in 1793, when the governor of the Spanish colony *La Florida* dispatched a secret mission in search of an advance guard of British Loyalists. The secret mission found the homestead of Bahamians Surles and Frankee Lewis and their family. Centuries before, Tequesta Indians had lived throughout southeast Florida. They relied on New River for hunting and fishing, and they utilized it as a transportation artery between the eastern Everglades and the Atlantic.

In fact, the first known documentation of New River is the *America Septentrionalis* map of 1631, on which the label "*R. Novo*" appears in Latin. Exactly why and by whom this waterway was named New River remains unproven. Many modern-day historians attribute the name to the river's frequently shifting Atlantic inlet, which has changed locations at least three times. One of the intriguing mysteries of New River—one that could explain its name—comes from a story that is said to have been passed down by generations of aboriginal Floridians. In that story, Natives, likely the Tequesta, witnessed the overnight birth of a new river.

The City of Fort Lauderdale was born on the banks of New River. Today, Fort Lauderdale is home to about 180,000 people. It is the seat of Broward County, the second-most-populous county in the state with about 2 million residents. Most people overlooking the sea-walled New River from their waterfront mansions, high-rise office buildings, and condominiums; while cruising on paddle-wheeled tour boats, mega yachts, and runabouts; when dining at its waterfront restaurants; or while strolling its Riverwalk have little or no idea of its ancient story. Some may have experienced a little of New River's more recent past in its historic district, which fronts the river beside Flagler's railroad tracks and is anchored by the Fort Lauderdale Historical Society and the 1905 New River Inn. Near the historic district is the site of the old town's Indian trading post, which is now home of Stranahan House.

A story that goes untold on New River's tour boats is that of the killing of a pioneer's family on the river by a group of vengeful Seminoles. For decades, that event has been the source of speculation and misunderstanding. I first became intrigued with New River because of this story, which has been circulating since the early 1900s and is still around today. That story says that members of *my* family were murdered on New River's banks, leading to one of the river's historic neighborhoods being named Colee Hammock. As I began my research on what the Daughters of the American Revolution and City of Fort Lauderdale had memorialized as the "Colee Massacre," I found that, while much has been written about New River as parts of larger histories in books, magazines, and journals, the river's history has never been pulled together as one interconnected story. My goal with this book is to tell that story in a concise, easy-to-read fashion.

Legends and Lore of Fort Lauderdale's New River places the river as the central character in a story that spans hundreds of years. From this book flow the stories of early Native Floridians who hunted and foraged on the narrow strip of dry land between the Everglades and the Atlantic. They were joined in the late 1700s by immigrants from the Bahamas, Cuba, and elsewhere, as well as escaped slaves. Soon, white pioneers began migrating south either from or through the Spanish colonial region around St. Augustine, a distance of about three hundred miles over inhospitable terrain filled with voracious mosquitoes, snakes, panthers, bears, and other wildlife.

In reading this book, I hope you will find the same fascination I felt with a story of south Florida's rugged first settlers—Natives, Whites, and Blacks—living and trading together in relative harmony. I hope you will flash back with me to a time when travel was on horseback or wagon, over paths trod down by Natives long ago; a time when Fort Lauderdale's first real estate developers—including a strong-willed woman who convinced Flagler to relocate the path of his railroad and changed the route of today's U.S. 1—carved a new town out of the wilderness; a time when Broward County's namesake fostered development west of today's I-95, spawning swampland sales scandals led by a dapper developer named Dicky Bolles and instigating environmental problems that still plague the southern half of the peninsula.

While many of the stories around New River have either been confirmed or debunked, some will likely forever remain myths and mysteries.

ACKNOWLEDGEMENTS

Writing is like the evolution of a river, which generally begins with drops of water from the sky, pulled by gravity to the earth. Some drops feed the earth beneath, some evaporate back to the sky, and others begin a journey toward sea level, the oceans. As the drops congregate, they form small tributaries, combine into larger creeks and streams, and then become rivers. Water runs downhill, even in the seemingly flat land of south Florida.

So it is with a book. It began with an idea, the "drops of rain" in the analogy. The gravity that tugs at it is curiosity. The tributaries are writers and researchers, who combine ideas and create spoken or written thoughts that become articles, books, and blogs. The final destination is the reader—the ocean. Then the cycle begins again.

This book has many tributaries.

Patrick Scott is a valued contributor and one of the few advance readers of this manuscript. He commented, in particular, about how important three newspapermen were; they preserved many of the raindrops, the stories, before they were combined to form tributaries of articles and books to be written by others, some acknowledged herein. The reporters he mentioned were Agnew Welsh of the original *Miami News*, Wesley Stout of the *Fort Lauderdale Daily News*, and Bill McGoun of the *Miami Herald*'s Broward edition. One of the streams that formed from their early work was *Broward Legacy*, the magazine of the Broward County Historical Commission. Fifty-eight editions were published between 1976 and 2012. This magazine is a treasure-trove of local history, and it is now archived online. Without that resource, I could not have written this book.

Acknowledgements

My first personal acknowledgement is to the late Dr. Michael Gannon, a distinguished professor emeritus of history at the University of Florida and my godfather, who inspired and mentored me to write my first book, *Towers in the Sand: The History of Florida Broadcasting*. Mike's guiding hand and rich voice was with me as I wrote this book.

Robert Gold, a professor emeritus of history, took me under his wing after critiquing *Towers in the Sand* for the *St. Augustine Record*. He encouraged me to write more, then helped me find the stream that became this book. Patricia Zeiler, the executive director of the Fort Lauderdale Historical Society, enthusiastically supported the project, helped connect me with other contributors, and personally augmented the photographs contained herein. Patrick Scott spent countless hours helping me navigate the available body of research and provided me with thoughtful guidance about the hurtful term *massacre*, causing me to use it sparingly and only in context.

Rodney Dillon and Barbara Poleo were early and continuing contributors—in facts, nuance, and editing. Seth Bramson, through his immense knowledge, experience, and vast collection of treasures, brought inspiring enthusiasm to the book and provided detailed editing.

Bill Crawford, who first made me aware of the true role my family played in Florida's progress through his articles and book, *Florida's Big Dig*, shared his insight and experience. Erin Purdy, who was, at the time, the chief archivist of the Broward County Historical Archives, went above and beyond to help this novice researcher discover hidden gems in files, folders, and online from her collections and elsewhere.

Engineers Tyler Chappell and Charlie Isiminger helped me understand the science behind the stories, and Charlie introduced me to another engineer, Tom Tepper, who confirmed the feasibility of an ancient story. Jim Welch, whose grandparents settled in Fort Lauderdale in 1917, provided me with immense local knowledge and captained his boat for my fact-finding cruise up New River through its south fork.

Terri Bailey created beautiful maps and illustrations that help connect old stories with modern locations and add immeasurably to the readers' experience. Joe Gartrell, my acquisitions editor at The History Press, was my guide through the writing process. It was a job well done on his part with consideration and humor. Ashley Hill's keen eye and cultural sensitivity improved the manuscript through her editing.

My wife and best friend, Martha, is my navigator through life and my books. From the first concept, through many drafts, hours of reading, thoughtful discussions, insightful editing, encouragement, and the patience of an oyster, she helped bring my books to fruition.

Legends and Lore of Fort Lauderdale's New River is the product of the good work of everyone I have mentioned—and many others who are known of and appreciated by me. Whatever success it achieves is due in large part to them; whatever shortcomings are my own.

1

THE LEGEND OF
HIMMARSHEE

There is a Seminole Indian legend, handed down through generations of peoples long forgotten, that "Beautiful New River came in a night." That where this mysterious river now traces her course to the sea one time was wild tropical jungles or pine forests. That the tribes then living in their palm thatched huts in these dark forests had gone to their rest in peace after the day's hunt when they were awakened by thundering noises and the earth trembling beneath them like the trembling of the deer when brought to bay by the hunter's dogs. Even the bravest of the tribe feared to venture forth until the great Spirit again smiled in the sunshine of the new day.

On venturing forth the next morning, a mighty and majestic river flowed through the forest in front of their then "Humpolee" (Home by the River). The tribe called this water "Himmarshee," (the New Water), which has since been changed by the white settlers…to "New River."[1]

If one were to ask modern-day residents and visitors of the booming city of Fort Lauderdale how New River got its name, they would likely get a shrug. Some may assume it was due to one of the massive dredge-and-fill projects that created vast acres of valuable waterfront real estate along the river's 165 miles of canals and the promotional moniker "the Venice of America." That notion is reinforced aboard the tour boats that travel the river with passengers ogling the multimillion-dollar homes of residents, both famous and not, and the mammoth yachts docked on the sea-walled New River.

Then there is the intriguing story that was previously recited of ancient Natives experiencing "the earth trembling beneath them" and the birth of a majestic *Himmarshee*, which is believed to be their word for "new water." There is much we don't know about the legend. No one knows precisely when or by whom the legend was originally disseminated. Some say the area's first schoolteacher, Ivy Julia Cromartie, taught it to her students around 1899. From then, it is said that the legend remained in relative obscurity until it resurfaced and gained a modicum of authenticity with its publication in the February 18, 1921 edition of the *Fort Lauderdale Sentinel*, a decade after the Town of Fort Lauderdale was officially recognized by the Florida legislature. Headlined "The Wonderful Legend of New River," the newspaper article (which appeared without a byline) supplemented the legend with a couple definitive statements:

> *Geologists who have made examination of the rocks of the coral ridge and those who have investigated all the legends and stories as well as the later history of the river say that the legend is* **probably true in every particular** *[emphasis added].*
>
> *Geologists believe that this was once an underground river through the coral ridge, the subterranean outlet for the waters of the Everglades and, at the time of some long-past earth convulsion, the rocks above gave way, and the "Himmarshee" moved majestically through the sunshine to be absorbed in the great bosom of the ocean.*[2]

We don't know why the editors of the *Sentinel* chose to publish the story on that particular date in 1921. A review of the entire newspaper does not show any specific event or action that would have precipitated its publication, save for two lengthy and romantic poems written about New River by ladies from up north.[3] A plausible explanation is that, at ten years old, Fort Lauderdale was looking for something distinctive about itself.

The Roaring Twenties was a period of rapid industrial growth, advances in technology, increased productivity and wages, and a growing middle class with cash in its pockets. It was an economic boom—a tide raising all ships—and waterfront Fort Lauderdale was no exception. The town was in the midst of exceptional growth in agriculture, commerce, real estate, and tourism. The wharves along New River were packed with produce that was shipped from the Everglades on specially designed boats via the North New River Canal to be transported on Henry Flagler's Florida East Coast Railway to kitchens up north. The opening of the First National Bank and the new chamber of commerce encouraged business growth. The Las Olas Causeway and bridge to the beach were complete, and the New River Inn and the recently opened Broward Hotel needed guests.

The town's already impressive group of civic leaders, including Philemon N. Bryan and his sons, Tom and Reed; Frank and Ivy Stranahan; Edwin T. King; and others, was supplemented by the 1919 arrival of Commodore A.H. Brook, a skilled publicist who became enthralled with the area and was actively involved in promoting it. What better than a mysterious story told by Indians to infatuate a nation?

While there is a lot we still don't know, we *do* know that Seminoles could not have witnessed the event. Despite their prominence in Florida culture today, the Seminoles are not indigenous to Florida. "The tribe was part of the Creek Confederacy in Alabama and Georgia for a far longer time and was a relatively late arrival on the peninsula," explained James W. Covington in *The Seminoles of Florida*, adding that the Apalachees, Calusas, Timucuans, Tequesta, and other tribes arrived much earlier. "The original tribes of Florida, which may have numbered as many as 100,000 persons, were virtually extinct when the Lower Creeks [who lived near the Florida border and would become known by Whites as Seminoles] began making permanent settlements on the peninsula in the latter half of the eighteenth century."[4] By that time, New River was well established.

Putting aside for a moment which Natives may have experienced it, could such an earth-altering event have occurred? An informed opinion comes from a lengthy article published in the *New River News* in 1984, a time when it was the official magazine of the Fort Lauderdale Historical Society. The author, Fort Lauderdale native Bill Raymond, was a marine geologist and chairman of the Marine Archaeological Advisory Council of the Broward County Historical Commission. He compared the legend with what was then known about southeast Florida's ancient geology. While acknowledging that the Seminoles could not have witnessed the event, Raymond wrote that "there [was] strong evidence" that an overnight event, such as the one described in the legend, could have happened.[5]

To understand how Raymond came to that conclusion, it is first necessary to understand New River's ancient role as one of just a few outlets for fresh water flowing from central Florida, to Lake Okeechobee, to the Everglades, and then out to the Atlantic Ocean and Gulf of Mexico. One must first think about the peninsula's terrain. North of Orlando, there are gently rolling hills, but traveling south, Florida's interior is flat as a pancake, with only a slight slope toward the south.

The natural flow of water began in earnest just south of Orlando in Osceola County's chain of lakes, merging into a one-to-two-mile-wide floodplain known as the Kissimmee River Basin. In its natural state, the Kissimmee River, which is fed by surface rainwater instead of springs or subterranean rivers, meandered over one hundred miles, an as-the-crow-flies distance of just fifty miles, before flowing into Lake Okeechobee. In the rainy season (from May to October), the river overflowed into the basin, continuing its southerly flow.

On reaching Lake Okeechobee, its journey was still not complete. The lake is immense. It is the tenth-largest lake in the United States, but it is exceptionally shallow—just nine feet deep on average.[6] Historically, Lake Okeechobee has not been the confined body of water that it is now. It was once part of an ancient system of natural water flow. Think of Lake Okeechobee as a shallow bowl on the north side of a larger shallow bowl— the larger being the Everglades. Both bowls are composed of limestone, with the Okeechobee bowl tilted slightly to the south. In the rainy season, when storm clouds emptied over the Kissimmee River Basin and the lake, the accumulation of water was too great; Okeechobee overflowed its southern limestone rim into the larger but still shallow Everglades bowl. From there, the flow continued its slow migration south. Eventually, the water bumped against, then overflowed, the narrow limestone rim of the Everglades bowl. Over centuries, the water wore away the limestone, cutting channels that led to the Gulf of Mexico and the Atlantic Ocean.[7]

One of those ancient channels became what is now called New River, the major drainage outlet for the southeastern Everglades basin that carries overflow from the sawgrass to the ocean. "Sections of this channel appear to have remained constant through the centuries," Raymond wrote, noting that "some portions are 200 feet deep, where the river cut into the older rock strata during the lowered sea levels of the Pleistocene ice ages [about 2.6 million years ago]."[8] It is conceivable that, as Florida emerged from the lowering sea, the deep channel became an underground river that may have been exposed later in some geologic or seismic event.

Raymond's article concludes: "Geologic evidence suggests that the legend of New River could indeed be true. Was it, or did it spring from Seminole folklore of tribes long ago or from the vivid imagination of an early settler? We may never know."

When Bill Raymond's article was published in 1984, the original IBM personal computer had just turned three years old and the internet was in its infancy; thus, an easily accessible body of knowledge was limited. There was no Google. With advances in accessing information, geological testing, and the vertical development of downtown Fort Lauderdale, does Raymond's theory stand the test of time?

To find out, the author of this book sought a modern-day expert. Tom Tepper is a geotechnical engineer with over fifty years of experience—most of it dealing with the complex geology of south Florida. He was most recently a partner in Dunkelberger Engineering and Testing, now a part of Terracon Consultants. In the late 1990s and 2000s, he did an extensive amount of geological work as part of the high-rise construction boom in downtown Fort Lauderdale, and he therefore brings a twenty-first-century perspective to Raymond's article.

In summary, Tepper agrees that, based on the geology and hydrodynamics of the area, there is reason to believe that the story told in the Native legend could have happened. "If you look at the geology of downtown Fort Lauderdale, there is a layer of carbonate rocks [limestone] five or six feet below the ground surface, extending down as much as twenty to twenty-five feet," Tepper explained in a 2019 interview with the author.

The layer is made of Miami limestone, which is composed mainly of ooliths, small rounded grains that look like fish eggs intermixed with some quartz sand and fossils.[9] The layer is not solid, like poured concrete; rather, it is composed of large and small rocks that have become packed together over millennia. As such, water can seep around the rocks, eventually becoming a flow of water—an underground river encased in caverns with a thin limestone ceiling just under the ground surface. Tepper explained that this is significant. Citing an article in the *Journal of the Geotechnical Engineering Division* of Georgia Tech, he noted that the groundwater in south Florida has a slight acidity, a natural phenomenon that occurs when grasses and other vegetation of the Everglades decay. Carbonate materials, such as limestone, are soluble in water that is slightly acidic. The primary effect of solubility is an increase in the porous nature of the rocks, further enhancing water circulation. The acidic water changes the characteristics of the limestone rocks and causes them to resemble swiss cheese or hardened, brittle sponges. This can happen in a short period of time—during a human lifetime.[10]

While the geology of the New River area is proven, could a seismic event such as an earthquake cause the exposure of an underground river? According to the Florida Department of Environmental Protection, there have been "only twenty-four 'seismic events' in Florida," and "it's likely that just five were actual earthquakes."[11] Florida has also been impacted, to some degree, by earthquakes outside the region. For example, in 1880, there were two specific notations of an earthquake in Cuba being felt in Florida.[12] Wikipedia lists twenty-three "notable" earthquakes in Cuba since 1578 but adds that the island experiences an average of about two thousand seismic events each year. In 2014, an earthquake just off the northern coast of Cuba shook buildings in Miami and frightened residents as far north as Jacksonville.[13] In January 2020, Miami high-rises swayed and were evacuated as a powerful earthquake struck between Cuba and Jamaica.[14] It is therefore reasonable to assume that, if the Natives camped at the right place at the right time, they could have felt "the earth trembling beneath them," as described in the legend, and the brittle swiss-cheese ceiling of an underground cavern could have collapsed and revealed a New River before them.

Others have offered alternatives to an earthquake. Dr. Cooper Kirk, the first county historian of the Broward County Historical Commission, suggested "a catastrophic head of water," perhaps from an extremely wet hurricane, could have cut through the narrow rock rim of the Everglades, creating or altering existing rivers.[15] Harry A. Kersey Jr., a professor of history at Florida Atlantic University and the author of several books, including *The Stranahans of Fort Lauderdale*, suggested that "torrential rains" could have caused the earth to tremble, perhaps exposing an underground river that existed "eons ago."[16] Either theory, combined with the area's geology, could have created the event that is memorialized by the Native legend.

Further evidence of the rocky, cavernous base on which today's downtown Fort Lauderdale sits were at least two whirlpools, one at New River's sharp turn at Sailboat Bend and the other farther east at Tarpon Bend. The whirlpools, said by some to be 90 to 125 feet deep, provided hours of entertainment for children growing up on New River. Numerous writers, including those of the 1921 *Fort Lauderdale Sentinel* article referenced earlier, told stories of boards that had been thrown into the Sailboat Bend whirlpool being sucked down, only to resurface some two miles downriver at Tarpon Bend. The deep holes were also documented in the 1870 field notes of pioneer surveyor Marcellus Williams; he told of "deep caverns in

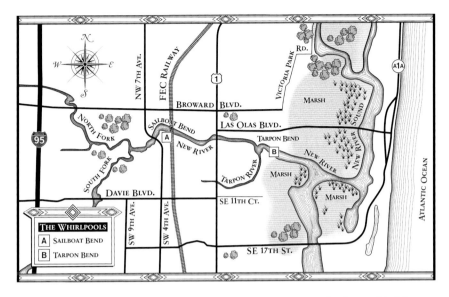

The mysterious New River whirlpools with today's major streets and railway added for reference. *Illustration by Terri Bailey, base map courtesy of the Dolph Map Company.*

the coral rock" where the current was so strong it was nearly impossible to propel a boat with oars.[17]

Robert H. Gore III, a marine biologist and grandson of R.H. Gore Sr., a former publisher of the *Fort Lauderdale News*, grew up on New River in the 1940s. While dismissing the Native legend as "pure fiction" in an article written in 1996, he wrote fondly of the locally famous whirlpools, presuming they were "caused by fresh water draining down through an opening in the limestone" beneath the river. "The vortices for all of these whirlpools appear to be most turbulent at low tide," he wrote, "adding support to the supposition that the river water was draining out to sea through limestone sinkholes in the river bottom."[18] Today, the whirlpools are no more—the caverns are filled with sediment from the early twentieth-century efforts to drain the Everglades.

———

RETURNING TO THE QUESTION of who may have witnessed the event that exposed a new river and gave it its name: if not the Seminoles, then who? Most researchers agree that it was probably the Tequestas (pronounced and sometimes spelled "Tekesta"), who could have been in the right place at the right time to experience the event. They settled in today's southern Palm Beach, Broward, and Miami-Dade Counties. Following the traditions of their ancestors, the Tequesta "clustered on the coasts, especially on estuaries where fresh water could be obtained and along the higher inland ridge that parallels the coast in southeast Florida," explained Jerald T. Milanich, an anthropologist and archaeologist who specializes in Native American culture in Florida.[19] The discovery of Native American artifacts that date back as early as AD 1200 in the area of New River's Tarpon Bend reaffirms the likelihood that Tequestas lived along its banks. It is also conceivable that the Tequestas' story was handed down to the Seminoles (thus the reference in the legend to "generations of people long forgotten"), who then repeated it.

There is another less intriguing explanation for the name New River. Over the centuries and continuing today, the clockwise movement of sand along the lower East Coast of the United States, known as "littoral drift," moves sediment predominantly southward. Today, one can see the effect of this drift at jetties, where sand piles up on the north side and erodes on the south side. Natural inlets had no jetties; with incoming tides, the sand was carried inland, creating shoals and sometimes closing the inlet. "Tropical storms and nor'easters also battered and weakened the shoreline, closing inlets and opening others," wrote Kersey. "Thus, the New River Inlet has been changed frequently by the whim of nature, as numerous maps attest."[20] This relocating inlet could have caused travelers and surveyors to call it a "new river."

———

REGARDLESS OF WHETHER THE name New River was born of an earthshaking Native experience or a shifting inlet, even that long-accepted moniker was not sufficient for some who were seeking more promotional pizzazz. Gore, the straight-talking grandson of a newspaperman, wrote, perhaps with a little scolding, "During the boom days of the late 1920s, the city chamber of commerce proposed renaming the river 'Himmarshee-hatchee,' an unlikely combination of two Seminole words that reputedly meant 'New Water River.'" It didn't take, and the ancient New River remains so named today.[21]

MYSTERIOUS *PAY-HAI-OKEE*

NEW RIVER'S SOURCE, SEMINOLES' SALVATION

New River owes its existence to *Pay-hai-okee*, known by the White man as the Everglades, the mysterious wetlands and marshes that originally composed most of the southern half of the Florida peninsula. The name "Everglades" has American heritage; it first appeared on a map shortly after Spain ceded its territory, *La Florida*, to the United States in 1819. But even though it had a new name, it had little identity to the White men who then proclaimed its ownership. No one had "owned" the Everglades before.

The aboriginal people we now call Native Americans, perhaps just a few dozen, entered the region today known as Florida about twelve thousand years ago. They were nomads, constantly moving in search of food. The land they found looked far different than it does today. To begin with, the land mass was about twice its present size, and the air was much cooler and drier. That's because a vast amount of the world's water was still encased in enormous glaciers—the last vestiges of the ice ages—that had been formed over two million years earlier and were just beginning to thaw. Sea levels were much lower; as a result, land masses were much larger than they are now. In fact, Fort Lauderdale, if it had existed then, would have been miles from the beach and as much as three hundred feet above sea level.[22]

The Natives first inhabited the thick woodlands in the panhandle and northern peninsula, areas that were rich in wildlife, pure in water, and abundant in berries, nuts, mushrooms, and greens to forage. And they were virtually alone, without enemies or strange diseases. They were peaceful and content, and they multiplied. "As human populations increased and as

LEGENDS & LORE OF FORT LAUDERDALE'S NEW RIVER

the climate of Florida became more like it is at present, the native societies also changed," wrote Milanich. By about 3000 BC, the warmer and wetter conditions supported modern vegetation, and as their tribes grew, they broadened their horizons toward the south.[23]

They roamed land without fences, bound only by the natural earth and rising sea level. They gathered in various regions where food was abundant, developing over centuries their own unique cultures. They are believed to have lived in southeast Florida beginning in about 500 BC, and two millennia later, they could well have been gazing at the ocean when the white sails of the ships carrying Juan Ponce de Leon and other conquistadors peeked over the horizon.

We don't know how the ancient Native Americans referred to themselves; the names we call them today were given to them by early explorers. The Spanish assigned the name "Tequesta" to the Indians living on the coast of today's Palm Beach, Broward, and Miami-Dade Counties. They made their villages on the high ridge a few miles inland from the Atlantic; from there, they had access to a virtual smorgasbord of food. On the densely wooded pine ridge where they made their camps, they hunted deer, rabbit, and turkey. Where the trees were thin, the Tequestas harvested the thick roots of the cycad fern *Zamia pumila*, pounding them and washing away deadly toxins to produce a flour they called "compte" that later White settlers would call "coontie." From the coontie, they made bread and a gruel, "sofkee," staples of the Native diet. A canoe trip to sandbars in the bay on an outgoing tide could yield baskets of "fat fish" (black drum), which they trapped via a system of primitive but effective dams and weirs.[24]

The Natives explored warm inshore waters like New River and found incredible species of fish ready for their woven nets; they also found slow-moving manatees, larger than big men, that provided enough food for a village. On calm days, they hauled their canoes over the narrow barrier island to the Atlantic in search of sharks and other fish of all varieties and seagoing turtles—green, leatherback, loggerhead, and hawksbill. From the beach, they gathered turtle eggs and treasures of the ocean—shells by the millions, sharks' teeth, driftwood from far-away storms, and, later, materials from shipwrecks of early explorers and slave raiders.

A couple of miles west of their villages, on the high ridge, there opened a vast, flat expanse of shallow water that was mostly obscured by sawgrass that was as tall as ten feet and some four thousand years old. Protruding from the sawgrass were—and still are—islands of various sizes, some with no more vegetation than gnarly brown bushes. Cypress domes break the

Tequesta brave harvesting "Bounty from the Sea." *Painting by Theodore Morris, floridalosttribes.com.*

skyline, the trees growing in depressions in the limestone bedrock. The tallest trees are rooted in the deepest water, and the tree heights taper off to the shortest trees around the edges in shallow water, mirroring the limestone bowl below. Around the islands and beneath the sawgrass, the water flows almost imperceptibly down a soft southbound slope, supporting an abundance of life. On the small islands, flocks of egrets, white and glossy ibises, and blue herons feed their young from passing schools of fish. Alligators and crocodiles bask on the banks or swim leisurely until aroused into frenzy by an easy meal. (South Florida is the only place in the United States where these species coexist.)[25]

Because they were nomads, the Natives readily adapted to their surroundings. They exchanged the rough animal skin clothing of their former cold climates "for cooler things in this country of the sun," wrote Marjory Stoneman Douglas in *The Everglades: River of Grass.* "The moss of the trees made excellent light skirts for the women, who did their work more freely with nothing above the waist." The men fashioned loincloths from palmetto strips on a belt "and tied a bunch of moss on behind, not for decency, but to have something more comfortable to sit on than bare skin and bones." Douglas also wrote that young warriors exchanged the moss hanks for raccoon tails, which were considered "very soft, very dashing."[26]

South Florida was a land without flint, metal, or hard rocks. Fire was made by rubbing sticks. Adaptation was a way of life ingrained into the Natives' DNA. Hard shells on the beach, especially lefthanded conch and large queen conch, could be transformed into hammers, spades, and picks. Smaller shells made excellent drinking cups. Sharks' teeth set into wooden handles made sharp knives for cutting meat and carving intricate patterns on pottery. Fish bones became hairpins. Little went to waste.

By all accounts, they were a happy lot, traversing from pine ridge, to ocean, to grassy water, and back again whenever they pleased. As told by Douglas:

> *The brown, healthy, almost naked people, smeared with fish oils to keep off the mosquitoes or the sandflies, laughed and joked about the great cooking fires. Their careless hard heels trampled into the sand and ashes the bones, the discarded shells and all the leavings of their untidy roving lives. They came back again and again to the same feasting places. The piles they built up through centuries are called kitchen middens, refuse heaps which in time became accumulations of rich black dirt, with broken bits of their pottery and pieces of shells and bones.*[27]

Then came the strangers.

Although absent from the unwritten languages of the Natives, the word *strangers* is probably a fitting description of the people who showed up uninvited at their camp sites and hunting grounds. The Natives' first encounter with these strangers may have been just after the turn of the sixteenth century, when Spain launched an ever-widening circle of voyages from its bases in the Caribbean Sea, according to preeminent Florida historian Michael Gannon. Some were slaving expeditions to replenish laborers in Spain and Cuba, where indigenous populations were dying off due to harsh work practices and European diseases. "Probably one or more of those expeditions happened upon the Florida peninsula," Gannon wrote.[28]

Around the same time, Juan Ponce de Leon, the former governor of Puerto Rico, received a charter to conquer and claim the island of Bimini for the Spanish Crown. He departed from Puerto Rico with a flotilla of three small ships on March 3, 1513. His ships were carried north by the Gulf Stream, the powerful current that was unknown by Ponce and other early explorers, to a landfall "just south of Cape Canaveral, near Melbourne Beach," according to Gannon.[29] The location of that historic landfall is the subject of debate that continues to this writing. Some authorities place it farther north. Ponce de Leon may have thought he had actually landed on the island of Bimini, which is known today as a tiny piece of land but was believed by early explorers to be quite large. Regardless, most historians agree that Ponce de Leon named his discovery *La Florida*, the Spanish term for "flowery," due to its lush vegetation and the fact that he discovered it during Eastertime or *Pascua Florida*.

Gannon's account says that when Ponce de Leon first went ashore to take formal possession for the Spanish Crown, he encountered no indigenous people. After a six-day rest, the small fleet sailed south, where it soon encountered the force that had unknowingly transported it northward—the Gulf Stream. Ponce de Leon barely noticed it when he sailed west, but then, hitting it head on, "his ships were propelled backward, even though they had wind abaft the beam." Heading toward shore to break free of the rushing warm water stream, the fleet anchored at a cape near what is today's Lake Worth Inlet, and on sighting some Natives, the crewmembers went ashore to make contact. It did not go well. The Natives attacked the party with tomahawks and war clubs. Escaping with minor wounds, the Spanish quickly returned to their ships and sailed north to Jupiter Inlet to take on firewood and water, "only to be attacked again by a larger party of sixty men." This time, Ponce de Leon nabbed a warrior to be his guide for the rest of the voyage. Sailing south again, hugging the shore to avoid the Gulf Stream, Ponce de Leon continued his journey, eventually rounding the Keys and entering the Gulf of Mexico.[30]

There is no known written record of why the Natives reacted so violently to the strangers. Perhaps it was because of their own history of intertribal warfare or their natural fear of these humans and their large, tall-masted ships. This violence was more likely due, however, to the recent vicious attacks by slavers, who captured men, women, and children and carried them off, never to be seen again. That was the beginning of the end of the Natives of Florida. Within two hundred years, "warfare, slave trading, and especially epidemics of disease had annihilated what had been a population of some 350,000 people at the time Ponce de Leon first came to Florida," wrote Milanich.[31]

While the aboriginal Floridians were being decimated, new tribes were arriving in north Florida from Georgia and Alabama. These new immigrants, the Lower Creeks, fatigued from fighting the larger tribes of the Creek Confederacy, sought to establish new lives for themselves by initially settling in the mostly vacant land between Pensacola and St. Augustine. The Spanish gave them their name: Seminole. Some historians attribute the name to the Creek term *simano-li*, or "separatist," and the Spanish word *cimmaron*, or "runaway." Others say it meant "outlaw" or "wild people." According to Marjory Stoneman Douglas, the Natives didn't like the name imposed on them, preferring to call themselves *Ikaniuksalgi*, meaning "the people of the peninsula."[32] One seldom sees that name today.

It was the Seminoles who named the Everglades *Pay-hai-okee*, their expression for "grassy water." They brought with them important aspects of their former Creek life, including tribal ceremonies with the smoking of peace pipes. Many of the ceremonies were centered on the purification and spiritual rejuvenation brought forth by drinking *asi*, the "black drink." Its primary ingredients were the berries of holly trees, which are native to the South; they were brewed to make a tea-like strong, dark concoction that was to be consumed quickly and completely from gourds. Combined with other herbs, it was so emetic that, after drinking, the men quietly left the tribal square to vomit, cleansing their bodies from impurities and evil spirits, leaving behind only courage and strength. That ritual was often repeated by warriors before battle.

"They were, and are, a hearty people, with a great gusto for living," wrote Douglas in 1947. "They loved feasts and dances. There was the harvest dance in the fall, when they paid respect to the flesh animals by which they lived, imitating the way they moved and shook their heads, [howling and bellowing]."[33] In springtime, when new corn was growing, they celebrated the "Green Corn Dance," the most important and enduring of their ceremonies, lasting three days or more. Its rituals revolved around "purity, agricultural fertility, and maintaining the balance of the world," explained Milanich.[34] The festival is still celebrated today, although it has been witnessed by only a few non-Natives.[35]

The Seminoles also knew how to have fun and played stickball, a game handed down from their Creek ancestors. Similar to today's lacrosse, it involved hitting a ball sewn from deer hide with looped wooden rackets laced with skin thongs. The goal was to hit a consecrated post. This was played out in a fast and furious competition with few rules by competitors loosely organized in two teams. Douglas called it a kind of substitute for war. But unlike war, women often joined in the competition, using their tough-skinned open hands instead of sticks.

"For a half a century before Florida was transferred from Spain to the United States, Seminoles had prospered and their numbers increased tenfold," wrote John K. Mahon and Brent R. Weisman in *The New History of Florida*. Spain, having regained Florida from the British in 1784, after the American Revolution, had a tenuous hold over the immense, virtually untamed wilderness. The Seminoles had free rein to continue many of the actions they had learned as Creeks, including their lucrative trade with the newly immigrated White settlers who were eager to acquire products from the Natives' wilderness homes. The skins of deer they killed with bows and arrows were traded for guns and ammunition. Then, armed with these "fire sticks," the Natives widened their hunting grounds as far south as the Everglades. Eighteen pounds of skins could yield a new gun. Sixty pounds (achievable in a good year) could yield a new saddle.

"Not everything the Seminole supplied came from the forest." With the experience and skills of the slaves they harbored, many being runaways from productive plantations farther north, the Seminoles developed fields of corn, rice, watermelons, peaches, potatoes, and pumpkins. The Natives sold the crops to grocers in St. Augustine. Isolated as it was, America's oldest city was in perpetual need because of its growing population.[36]

With Seminole entrepreneurship came a gradual dissolution of the traditional tribal structure, which was centered on powerful chiefs who historically maintained order and discipline among and between large tribes. Over time, the Seminoles began living up to the Creek version of their "separatist" name.[37]

As noted earlier, the Seminoles depended, in part, on labor from escaped slaves for their Florida farms. Referred to as Black Seminoles, some of these escaped slaves were descendants of African-born slaves who had escaped plantations in the Carolinas and found refuge and honest work with the Spaniards of St. Augustine. In 1738, the Spanish governor rewarded them with a fortified Black settlement known as Fort Mose (pronounced "moh-SAY") just north of St. Augustine. It was the first legally sanctioned free Black town in the United States. In addition to providing farming skills to the Seminoles, the stronger of the freedmen proved to be able fighters.[38]

The combination of the Natives' relative economic prosperity, their harboring of runaway slaves, and the Spanish authority's laissez-faire attitude toward it all inflamed the English colonists. After the American Revolution, it also inflamed the fledgling United States government. Spanish Florida became not just a thorn in its side, but its enemy, and America focused its anger on the Natives.

In 1817, fresh from fighting the British in the Battle of New Orleans, U.S. Army general Andrew Jackson invaded Spanish Florida, targeting Seminole towns and plantations and encountering Native Seminoles fighting side by side with Black Seminoles. Despite the fact that Jackson's act was an illegal American invasion of foreign land, his campaign became known as the First Seminole War.

At the war's conclusion in 1819, Spain, realizing it could no longer avoid the inevitable, ceded Florida to the United States. Three years later, in 1822, Florida officially became a U.S. territory. Swarms of American settlers from Georgia and the Carolinas poured into the new territory, coveting the fertile lands occupied by the Seminoles while searching for runaway slaves under their protection. Conflicts were inevitable. The new territorial government's first attempt at solving the "Seminole problem" was the Treaty of Moultrie Creek in 1823. It was not so much a "treaty" as it was a "permit" for the United States to relocate the Seminoles to a four-million-acre reservation in central Florida, promising tools for farming, rations until they could sustain themselves, and cash incentives. According to the treaty, the Natives would have to give up claim to all lands outside the newly assigned reservation. Unstated but understood by the government was its belief that by corralling all the Natives in one place, it would be easier to round them up and ship them to the "Indian Lands" in today's Oklahoma.

Distrusting the federal government, only a few chiefs placed their mark of acceptance on the Treaty of Moultrie Creek. Those who did soon realized their mistake. Not only did they find much of the reservation unsuitable

The 1823 Treaty of Moultrie Creek, named for the small tributary of the Matanzas River south of St. Augustine, would have confined all Florida Native Americans to an isolated area in the center of the territory. *Illustration by Terri Bailey.*

for agriculture and absent of sufficient game, but it was also isolated from the coasts, eliminating an important food source and their opportunity to trade with Cuban fishermen as they had in Florida. The government quickly reneged on its promise to provide sufficient food and money. The Seminoles were starving. Their distrust of the White man was reaffirmed.

Matters, however, did get worse. Andrew Jackson's determination to rid the southeastern United States of Native Americans was rewarded when he was inaugurated president in 1829. A year later, after bitter disputes about the issue in Congress, Jackson prevailed and signed into law the Indian Removal Act of 1830, which authorized the government to grant land west of the Mississippi in exchange for existing Native lands, including the Florida reservation that was granted in the Treaty of Moultrie Creek.

In May 1832, Seminole leaders were summoned to meet with representatives of the U.S. Department of War to hear what was planned for them under the Indian Removal Act. They were told in no uncertain terms that they were going to be relocated, either voluntarily or by force. While there is no known documentation of precisely what was said, others testified that only after coercion, bribery, and deceit did fifteen Seminole leaders put their mark of acceptance on the Treaty of Payne's Landing. They were to be relocated within three years.

Most Seminoles remained steadfast in their refusal to leave what they considered to be their homeland; at the same time, the U.S. Army prepared to enforce the relocation. Skirmishes led to negotiations (during which the government generously offered food and whiskey that was eagerly partaken of by the Seminoles), which were followed by more skirmishes, more negotiations, more food, and more whiskey in a seemingly endless circle. All the while, the Seminoles' ranks increased. "By 1835, there were between 800 and 1,400 Indian warriors fragmented into numerous bands," reported Mahon and Weisman. "These warriors had 400 black men as allies, rated by whites as better fighters than the Indians. Each band had a hereditary chief, but there was still no principal chief over them all."[39] This lack of a unifying leader was a problem for the Seminoles, as individual bands operated unilaterally. Some chose to emigrate; others wanted to fight. But they did all of this without a large-scale plan.

That leadership void was filled by the son of a White father and a Creek mother. The boy's childhood name was Billy Powell, but after maturity, he was given the name Asi-yaholo from *asi*, the black drink of the Green Corn Dance, and *yaholo*, meaning the singer who served the drink to participants of the ancient ritual. The Whites called him Osceola. Never a chief himself, he instead led by the force of his personality; he galvanized the Seminoles to wage all-out war for their homeland. Some reports say he promised to fight "'til the last drop of Seminole blood has moistened the dust of his hunting ground."[40] Though lacking formal training, Osceola proved to be a skilled military tactician. Long before the battles escalated, "he persuaded the beleaguered chiefs to preserve their stockpiles of gun powder and ammunition," wrote U.S. Marine Corps major John C. White Jr., who analyzed the Second Seminole War from a modern military perspective in 1995. "He implemented a thorough reconnaissance of Fort King [near today's Ocala] and the military roads leading south." Osceola compiled information on the army's strength and the locations of their cannon battalions and bridges, which could have been choke points for ambushes.

Os-ce-o-la, the Black Drink, a Warrior of Great Distinction, painted by George Catlin at a fort near Charleston in January 1838. *Courtesy of the Smithsonian American Art Museum.*

His determination was brutal. "To discourage any more Indians from emigrating to the west, [Osceola] murdered Chief Charley Emathia, one of the original signatories [of the Payne's Landing Treaty]." He also said he would kill any Natives who continued to sell cattle to Whites.[41]

Instinctively, the Natives knew how to fight the United States, as it trained its army fighting orderly, face-to-face battles with the British. The Second

Seminole War was a guerrilla war fought in lightning-fast strikes by small groups of warriors who disappeared just as fast. Natives fought from behind trees and thick brush, in ditches, and, eventually, in the mysterious swamps and sawgrass of south Florida.

So mysterious were the Everglades that they weren't even detailed on the military maps of the day. John Lee Williams was an early authority on Florida's topography in its territorial days. He produced highly detailed maps and descriptions of the panhandle and the upper half of the peninsula, but when it came to publishing his 1837 map of the entire state, about one-third of the southern half was a blank slate, except for the words "Ever Glades" that arched from west to east. The map didn't even show Lake Okeechobee. Explaining the omission, Williams said the area had never been explored—meaning by White men with paper and pen. "Not one of the writers who have described this country since the change of flags [Spanish to U.S. territory] has been able to obtain any certain intelligence relating to this part of the peninsula."[42] That intelligence came while Williams's map was being printed; it did not come by men with paper and pen but by soldiers with guns and cannons in the Second Seminole War.

"Only the unbearable heat and humidity of the Florida climate exceeded the miserable features of the terrain," wrote military strategist Major White.[43] Having command of that terrain enabled a handful of Seminole chiefs with fewer than three thousand warriors to withstand the continued assaults of more than thirty thousand U.S. troops led by a succession of four generals and one colonel at a price tag of over $20 million.[44] The human toll was even greater:

- During the battle, 1,466 regular army soldiers died; 328 deaths were combat related, and the rest were due to illness and injury in the hostile environment. Seventy-four of the dead were officers.
- Just under 4,000 Seminoles were shipped to the new Indian Territory in the Midwest.

No one knows how many Seminole warriors, women, and children died in the battles.[45]

After seven miserable years, the Second Seminole War ended on August 14, 1842, not in victory for the United States or even a formal peace treaty, but with the resigned realization that the Seminoles would never entirely leave their homeland.

A Third Seminole War, three years in length, broke out in 1855, after more skirmishes broke out over slaves, land, and livestock, most instigated by the continued immigration of White settlers. At the conclusion of this war, only two hundred to three hundred Natives remained, cloistered in *Pay-hai-okee*. They were the ancestors of the proud Seminoles and Miccosukee who live peacefully and successfully in Florida today—unconquered.

3

NEW RIVER'S EARLY WHITE SETTLERS

Since the days of their ancestors, the Natives living in south Florida had had trade relations with visitors from the state's closest neighbors, the Bahamas and Cuba. After all, New Providence Island in the Bahamas was just 190 miles east of New River, and Havana was just 248 miles south. The Tequestas are said to have crewed Cuban fishing boats, exchanging their labor for fish and commercial fishing experience. It seems certain that some of those Bahamians and Cubans took up homesteads in south Florida, though few records exist.

The record is particularly clear about a British adventurist named William Augustus Bowles, who, as a teenager during the American Revolution, served as an English officer at the Pensacola garrison, only to be captured not by the revolutionaries, but by Creek Indians. While in their loose captivity, he developed a particular affinity for the Native people and a hatred of *La Florida*'s Spanish government for its treatment of them. After the revolution, he followed other loyalists to safe and compatible refuge in the Bahamas, which was then a British territory. From there, he returned to north Florida, where he lived with the Natives and married more than one. He eventually led the Natives in a quest to establish their own state. In 1788, Bowles, with a small army of Natives and some White Bahamians, attempted an insurrection, which was quickly and decisively quelled by the Spanish. Bowles escaped, ambition intact, and remained at large between the Bahamas and Florida, a burr under the Spanish saddle.

Provocateur William Augustus Bowles in Seminole Native garb. *Painting by Thomas Hardy, courtesy of the State Archives of Florida.*

In 1792, after rumors of more Bowles-affiliated insurgents gathering around New River in south Florida began to circulate, Spanish governor Juan Nepomuceno de Quesada felt compelled to take direct action. The problem? His Spanish government was weak, and its military was meager.

He knew that sending troops to investigate New River would have left St. Augustine vulnerable to other threats from the expansionist United States, Great Britain, France, and the troublesome Natives. His solution? Deception. He planned to send one of the small schooners that was regularly used to carry official documents to and from Havana on a clandestine mission with three handpicked spies to investigate who was living at New River and why. Its planning was top secret—St. Augustine was a leaking sieve of spies and loyalists of every persuasion.

The schooner, with its three secret agents, set sail on February 23, 1793. The cover story was logical: the three posed as commercial travelers from St. Augustine who were hitching a ride to Havana aboard the dispatch boat. They carried guns ostensibly to hunt game along the route. Their mission: to observe and report everything they could about the population and purpose of people on New River and to alert for any signs that Bowles might be planning another insurrection. Approaching New River Inlet (which was, at the time, located near today's Sheridan Street in Hollywood), the crew emptied the schooner's water casks into the sea—an excuse for coming inland. Towing the empty casks behind the boat, they crossed the sandbar and entered New River Sound on March 9; from there, they traveled north to the river's mouth, then upstream.

"It was a well-thought-out plan," wrote newspaper columnist and author Stuart B. McIver two centuries later. "The problem was timing." One of the primary subjects of the investigation, a Bahamian of English descent named Surles (sometimes written Surla or Charles) Lewis, his wife, Frankee, and their four grown sons, had sailed to New Providence Island a few days earlier. Their cargo, "fish oil extracted from sea creatures [Lewis] had harpooned and venison hams from deer that thrived in the woodlands near his home," was to be bartered for plantation supplies. He also planned to hoist a few with old friends in Nassau's taverns.[46]

Unaware that the target of their investigation was away, the governor's agents spotted a small house a couple of miles upriver on the south bank, near today's Sailboat Bend; then, they saw a barn, a blacksmith's shop, a chicken coop, a dock, and a house with a man coming out the front door, rifle in hand. Undaunted and consistent with their peaceful cover, they docked and greeted the rifleman, who identified himself as Captain Joseph Robbins. They told him they needed water. He believed them and said Lewis owned the house but that he and his family were in the Bahamas. Robbins, evidently a trusting man, told the undercover spies that he had been with Bowles on the 1788 attack on the Spanish

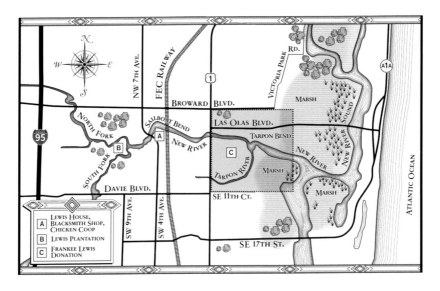

The Lewis family settlement in 1793. The Frankee Lewis Donation was granted after 1824.
Illustration by Terri Bailey, base map courtesy of the Dolph Map Company.

government but that he now lived peacefully on the river "with his mulatto wife, Rachel, their daughter, Susannah, and an American named Joel Radcliff." Robbins also told them that Lewis owned five horses, a gift from Bowles. "That evening, the governor's men dined on fresh-water trout cooked by Robbins' wife, and the agents, in turn, shared their wine, rum, and biscuits."[47]

Two days later, they were well fed, their investigations were complete, Lewis was still in the Bahamas, their cover story was still intact, and their water casks were full of fresh New River water, so the spies departed. Keeping with their story, when entering the Atlantic, they first sailed south, toward Havana, then turned out to sea. Once they were out of sight, they turned north toward St. Augustine.

Back home, the three spies dutifully reported their findings to Governor Quesada. Alarmed, he sent his report to the governor-general in Havana and recommended that the Spanish recruit a band of Natives to capture the families of Lewis and Robbins and turn them over to the government to be imprisoned as insurrectionists. "The report seems to have been buried under other documents of a more pressing nature, as the governor-general made no immediate reply to Quesada, other than to acknowledge receipt of the dispatch."[48]

No record has been found of Spanish government action based on the report; nor were there any acts, nefarious or otherwise, carried out by the Lewis or Robbins families. For the next three decades, the only other New River residents were presumed to be transient Bahamians "bent upon surviving by 'turtling,' fishing, shipbuilding, and 'wrecking.'"[49] ("Wrecking" was the term applied to the salvaging, and often looting, of shipwrecks.)

But remember, the record is sketchy. The Natives' history was oral, and the White settlers were often illiterate or didn't have the time, means, or inclination to document their lives—survival was the imperative. The colonial Spanish government kept detailed records, but "government" was nonexistent in the southern two-thirds of the peninsula. It wasn't until the Spanish cessation of *La Florida* to the United States in 1819 that somewhat reliable records were kept. Among the earliest recorded events in south Florida was an 1822 U.S. military reconnaissance mission that reported the Lewis men "had acted as pilots on the Florida reefs for many years," wrote Broward County historian and lawyer Patrick S. Scott. "Historians believed that Surles Lewis and his sons lived and died by the sea," except for one son, Jonathan, who survived to become an American citizen.[50]

What is well documented by Scott and others is that Frankee Lewis, who was by then Surles's aged and widowed wife, received a "donation" grant of one square mile of property (640 acres) in today's downtown Fort Lauderdale under an 1824 American law that was intended to benefit Protestant colonial settlers who could prove occupation and cultivation of the land prior to the Spanish government's cessation of Florida to the United States. The Spanish government had previously barred non-Catholics from land grants.[51] Even though she soon sold the Frankee Lewis Donation (twice, in fact, but that's another story), it would become a touchstone for written history and the future development of today's Fort Lauderdale.

About a year prior to the Lewis Donation, a transplanted Marylander established what would become a substantial New River homestead and, perhaps, south Florida's first manufacturing business. William Cooley arrived in *La Florida* in 1813, when he was around the age of thirty, and established a plantation at McGirt's Landing on the St. Marys River near the Georgia border. He later moved to Alligator Pond near present-day Lake City, where he "set about cultivating a small piece of land and trading with Indians who hardly were knowledgeable of white men's ways," according to Cooper Kirk. "Bold and often audacious in speech, he cultivated friendship with Indians led by Chief Micanopy," and he soon mastered their language. With a strong moral compass and knowledge of the law, he became deeply

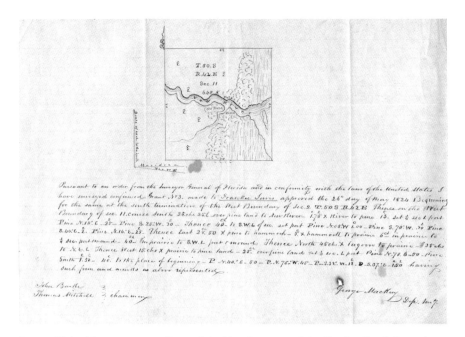

Deputy United States surveyor George MacKay documented the Frankee Lewis Donation in 1845; it was bound to the north by today's Broward Boulevard, west by U.S. 1, south by Southeast 11th Court, and east by the mangrove marsh. *Courtesy of History Fort Lauderdale.*

involved in a dispute regarding a Spanish man's claim to more than three hundred thousand acres of land that was in historically Native territory. Despite Cooley's representations on behalf of the Natives, the Spanish government upheld the man's claim, and when Florida became an American territory, the Spaniard converted his ill-gotten land into a fortune, selling to Anglo-Americans who were eager to exploit the new frontier.

Repulsed by what he felt was an illegal taking of Native lands, Cooley packed up his family and headed south, away from Spanish influence, and they settled in 1824 on the north bank of New River near the forks. Like other settlers, Cooley made no effort to buy the land but simply "squatted" there until Florida's new U.S. government established a formal ownership process through surveying and law.

The industrious Cooley immediately went to work building not only a home, but also an impressive manufacturing plant to process the thick roots of the two-to-three-foot-tall cycad ferns known by the Natives as coontie, which were abundant on the banks of New River. "The root is grated and squeezed and sifted to flour to make the thick watery gruel 'sofkee,' which

Florida Arrowroot (*Zamia*), a cycad known to the Native Americans as coontie. The underground roots were ground to detoxify and produce a fine flour used in cooking. *Image from* Useful Wild Plants of the United States and Canada *by Charles F. Saunders, 1920.*

was always the basis of Indians' diet here," wrote Marjory Stoneman Douglas.[52] (They did this despite the fact that, until processing, the root contains a deadly poison.) So prolific was coontie on New River that the Natives often called the body of water *Coontie Hatchee*.[53]

While the Natives relied on many busy hands to wash, pound, and sift the roots, removing the toxins and converting what remained to fine flour, Cooley's plant used New River's swift current to turn a water wheel, efficiently powering mechanical grinders and sifters in a twenty-seven-by-fourteen-foot structure. With its three-man crew, the plant could manufacture 450 pounds of coontie a day. The plant featured a fifty-foot wharf, where schooners were loaded with processed coontie for shipment to Key West, then on to northern and European ports. In addition to its domestic uses as an ingredient in bread dough and the Natives' watery gruel "sofkee," it was also used commercially as an ingredient in wafers and biscuits—staples aboard ships because of their non-spoiling characteristics. With the flour selling at eight to sixteen cents per pound, Cooley's coontie plant provided a handsome profit.[54]

Adjacent to his coontie plant, Cooley established a first-class homestead on New River, appropriate for an educated, cultured man and his family. His home was substantial for frontier days—a twenty-by-fifty-foot single-story, colonial-style structure built from cypress logs, sealing it against the weather, and floored with one-and-a-half-inch planks. The house was serviceably furnished and well supplied with fine Madeira wine, meat from Cooley's eighty hogs, and fresh vegetables grown on his twenty-acre farm. The view from the front porch was spectacular, as described by Cooper Kirk:

The river was crystal clear, except during the rainy season from May to October. Boasting perpendicular banks green to the water's edge, festooned with a profusion of wild grasses and shrubs, it varied in depth from three to twenty feet.....Numerous alligators sunned themselves on the sand spits located on the stream's lower end. An astonishing variety of fish could literally be had for the taking by the most novice of fishermen. Banks were usually clothed with pines, occasional hammocks of palmetto, water-oak, swamp maple, bay, Spanish oak and many other trees which stood silently, threaded with a growth of wild berries….Hardly bestirring himself from his piazza, Cooley could sight black bears, wildcats, wild turkeys, rabbits, turtles, deer, ducks, racoons, opossums and wild hogs, each capable of providing food and fiber in abundance.[55]

Continuing traditions from his life on the St. Marys River and having learned some of the local Natives' language, Cooley often invited the Seminoles who were camped on New River to join his family at their table, where they enjoyed generous meals, wine, and cigars, encouraging lively conversation.

Over the next few years, somewhere between forty and seventy persons, including slaves, settled around New River. Cooley was appointed the justice of the peace in 1831, making him the first official lawman and judge for Monroe County, which, at the time, stretched from Key West to just north of the St. Lucie River. (It wasn't until 1836 that Dade County was created.) At his New River home, he adjudicated disputes and assigned punishment for minor crimes—often with fines or whippings. He ordered serious offenders to be sent to the county seat in Key West for formal trials. His more mundane duties included appraising land, buildings, ships, slaves, and other pieces of property. By legislative action, Natives and Black people were subject to a different set of rules than the White settlers, including preemptive punishment, which usually involved whippings. "Although subscribing to southern sentiment, respecting the need to maintain strict surveillance over Indians and blacks, Cooley, on the whole, gained the respect of Indians, as he curbed the harshest white outbreaks," Kirk wrote.[56] In his growing community, Cooley's natural skills and affable personality led fellow residents to think of him as their trusted leader and friend.

Cooley's legal and business affairs often took him to Cape Florida (on today's Key Biscayne), Key West, and Havana; on these trips, he piloted his own ten-ton schooner and earned a reputation as a skilled mariner. These trips also led him to another part-time profession, "wrecking," which was the term applied to salvaging and, for some less-scrupulous practitioners, looting ships that became foundered along the shoal and reef-lined waters of Florida's east coast and the Keys. Until the shipping blockade of the Civil War sealed off the Florida coast, wrecking was the largest cash business along Florida's southeast coast. As early as 1832, newspapers in New York and New Orleans "claimed that wrecking on the Florida Reef…grossed over

$250,000 annually, an astronomical sum for the day," Kirk explained. "Some victims charged that wrecking consisted of nothing short of overt piracy," as more than a few rogue wreckers were known to provoke shipwrecks by moving markers and signal fires. With his nautical skills, Cooley became a wrecker; with his legal skills and sterling reputation, he received a territorial appointment as an appraiser of wrecked vessels and their cargoes, bringing some order and an aura of legitimacy to the practice.

Tropical storms and hurricanes—often called "gales" at the time—wreaked havoc on the lumbering ships of the nineteenth century, bringing big paydays for the wreckers who raced to their aid. Then came the awesome hurricane of September 1835. Frankee Lewis, whose memory of the area stretched almost half a century back, knew of no other storm that had such destructive power. So large and powerful was the storm that, when it came ashore in Key West, it toppled the newly constructed brick lighthouse at Ponce de Leon Inlet some three hundred miles up the coast. Almost every wrecking vessel in south Florida was disabled—all except for Cooley's.[57]

With no forewarning of the storm, the *Gil Blas*, a brand-new, two-hundred-ton Spanish brigantine en route to Spain from Cuba, sailed directly into its path, tossing ship, cargo, and crew onto the reef near Hillsboro Inlet. As

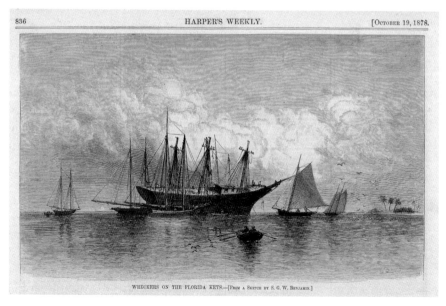

836   HARPER'S WEEKLY.   [OCTOBER 19, 1878.

WRECKERS ON THE FLORIDA KEYS.—[FROM A SKETCH BY S. G. W. BENJAMIN.]

Wreckers converge on a ship aground in the Florida Keys. *Drawing by S.G.W. Benjamin that accompanied an 1878 article in* Harper's Weekly, *courtesy Touchton Map Library, Tampa Bay History Center.*

soon as the storm cleared and the seas subsided, Cooley sailed his brig to the wreck and, at the instruction of its Spanish captain, loaded the valuable cargo of sugar and cigars onto his ship and transported it back to his New River home for safekeeping. The admiralty court in Key West ordered the ship (but not its cargo) to be sold at auction in December 1835. Cooley was engaged to refloat the *Gil Blas* and sail it back to Key West. High seas delayed the work.

As the year 1835 ended:

> *Cooley could survey with satisfaction the extent of his prosperity and the well-being he had achieved since his relocation to New River in 1824. He had been a Florida resident twenty-two years, eleven of them on New River. It was here that he probably met and married a woman who was formerly an Indian captive. Much younger than her husband, she bore him three children, two sons and one daughter. His empathy and admiration for Indians led him to name his sons Almonock and Montezuma after two of their chiefs. His daughter, now nearly eleven years old, and his nine-year-old son had excellent tutors in the persons of Mary E. Rigby and Joseph Flinton. His infant son still required the constant attention of his devoted mother.*[58]

Comfortable and confident on their New River estate, without the knowledge of what was happening elsewhere in Florida, William Cooley looked forward to a bright and prosperous year in 1836. Then, the unthinkable happened.

4

MYTH OF THE "COLEE MASSACRE"

I t is necessary to interrupt the story's timeline to fast-forward to March 16, 1934. On that day, the City of Fort Lauderdale and the Daughters of the American Revolution dedicated a monument to a tragic event on New River, and it was placed in a city park at Tarpon Bend. The bronze plaque read:

> *THIS MONUMENT MARKS SITE*
> *OF THE HISTORICAL*
> *COLEE MASSACRE*
> *WHICH EFFECTUALLY DESTROYED*
> *THE EARLIEST KNOWN WHITE*
> *SETTLEMENT ON NEW RIVER IN A*
> *SURPRISE ATTACK BY INDIANS*
> *FOLLOWING THE SEMINOLE INDIAN WAR*
> *1842*[59]

The only problem? That event didn't happen to that family, on that date, or in that location. Exactly how the story got started and endured is shrouded in family legend, the inexact genealogical research of the time, a lack of computers and the internet, unusual pronunciation, and, just maybe, the government and leaders of an ambitious city, trapped between the glitzy Flagler resorts of Palm Beach and the emerging real estate, tourism, and business mecca of Miami, seeking to establish its own promotable story. And promoted it was.

Fort Lauderdale mayor E.A. Pynchon had, by proclamation, declared the monument's dedication day a holiday and called for "all citizens and visitors to observe by attending the dedication exercises." He even suggested that citizens adorn their places of business and houses "with flags and other suitable decorations."[60] The *Fort Lauderdale News* noted that among the "men and women prominent in business and political circles in several states expected to attend" was Colonel Harold W. Colee, who was then the manager of the Florida Motor Lines (a forerunner of Greyhound), a director of the state chamber of commerce, and a member of the Florida governor's staff.[61] Colee was a descendent of the family that was being commemorated. Post-event newspaper coverage and personal memoirs noted the presence of a large contingent from the Daughters of the American Revolution, a group of Seminole Indians, and numerous other Colee family members from St. Augustine, where the Colee family originally settled. (As far as it is known, no one from the family lived in Fort Lauderdale at the time.) After the ceremony, honored guests were treated to tea at the New River home of Mrs. Frank Stranahan.[62]

Inspirational speeches by dignitaries may have been influenced by an unsigned document titled "Stone Will Recall Massacre by Indians," which can be found in the Research Library of the St. Augustine Historical Society. It says that George Colee and his family "sought to establish the first white settlement on New River in the Hammock which now bears his name [Colee Hammock]." The site he selected was choice Seminole farmland, "where, for years, they had raised their vegetables." Being forced off their land into the Everglades angered the Natives so much that they took revenge by massacring most of the family and burning their home, all while George Colee and his eldest son, James Louis, "were away in Key West for provisions." The family document explained that Colee had originally homesteaded near St. Augustine. He and his family left when one of their children contracted typhoid fever and remained away for about five years. Somehow, so the story went, they ended up at New River. The undated document includes future-tense references to the dedication ceremony and concludes with a past-tense listing of family members who were said to have attended.

The Colee Massacre story has been retold many times since—both in detail and anecdotally—by authoritative writers in various publications, including a 1936 booklet by the Federal Writers' Project (a program of President Franklin D. Roosevelt's New Deal), Marjory Stoneman Douglas's *Everglades: River of Grass* in 1947, and *Florida's Golden Sands* in 1950.[63] The

Left: Harold W. Colee in 1950, when he was the executive vice president of the Florida State Chamber of Commerce, Jacksonville. *Courtesy of the State Archives of Florida.*

Below: Stranahan House, circa 1910. *Courtesy of the State Archives of Florida.*

"Colee Massacre" commemorative plaque, which stood in Colee Hammock Park from 1934 until it was replaced with a historically correct plaque in 1971. *Courtesy of History Fort Lauderdale.*

author of this book, who is a direct descendent of George Colee, recalls being told of the massacre many times in his childhood.

Here is where the story of the massacre of George Colee's family starts to fall apart, according to contemporary research with the benefit of the worldwide resources of the internet, along with good work by many skilled and sharing local historians, journalists, and other current Colee family members. George Colee was born in London in 1801, and he worked as a painter for and befriended the family of William Riz, with whom he immigrated to the United States in 1821, arriving in Charleston.[64] The Riz family and Colee then settled in Picolata, Florida, on the St. Johns River eighteen miles west of St. Augustine. What attracted them to Florida is uncertain; however, they apparently arrived just prior to the United States' acquisition of the Spanish colony on July 17, 1821. Soon after, Riz was granted 640 acres of riverfront land in Picolata, presumably from the U.S. government land "donation" program that was discussed in chapter 3.[65] Less than a year later, Riz and his wife died of yellow fever. The land was apparently bequeathed to and equally split between Riz's son, William James Riz Jr. (who went by his middle name), and George Colee—a testament to the close relationship between the Riz family and Colee. That bond became even stronger when Colee married Riz's daughter, Tryphena, in 1828. He then acquired more land; established a homestead, farm, and family; and became a prominent member of the St. Augustine and Picolata communities.

⸎

THE DEBUNKING OF THE Colee Massacre story became public thanks to good investigative journalism by former *Saturday Evening Post* editor Wesley W. Stout, who, after retirement, moved to Fort Lauderdale, where he created a frequent column called "The Beachcomber" for the *Fort Lauderdale Daily News*. In the column, starting in 1954, Stout picked apart the myth of the Colee Massacre. To begin with, he pondered why an established and respected St. Augustine and Picolata pioneer would pack up his family, including a son with yellow fever, and trek almost three hundred miles through untamed, largely uninhabited wilderness to New River. Then, over the next six years, Stout meticulously researched, uncovered, and reported inconsistencies or just plain factual errors in the story, eventually concluding, "Every detail of the accepted story of the 'Colee Massacre' is wrong."[66]

Stout's articles caused quite an uproar in Broward County and the state's historical circles. As one can imagine, the articles also shocked the St. Augustine Colee family, who heretofore had continued to tell and write about the massacre, believing it to be fact.

The story then languished until 1973, when Bill McGoun of the *Miami Herald* resurrected it in his column, "Broward Heritage," adding to the body of evidence that the story was wrong.[67]

But, still, it lingered. In 1987, Rodney Dillon, who was then a special projects coordinator for the Broward County Historical Commission, attempted to bring all the known facts about the incident (as well as other local legends) into focus in one substantial article in the commission's official magazine, *Broward Legacy*. There, he disclosed the 1938 discovery by state librarian W.T. Cash of a collection of notices about the Second Seminole War. These notices documented that the actual date of the massacre was January 6, 1836, not 1842 as stated on the plaque. However, Cash still "maintained that the family killed was that of George Colee."[68]

53

Today, the contradictory articles are archived online and in historical research files, yet the legend of the Colee Massacre continues to occasionally resurface.

Perhaps the most convincing evidence that George's family did *not* die by the hands of Natives at New River are the following:

- Tryphena, George's wife, died in Picolata September 10, 1879, and was buried the next day in St. Augustine.
- James Louis died in St. Augustine in 1912.
- George A. died in St. Augustine in 1911.
- William Charles died in St. Augustine in 1923.
- Charles Henry died in Picolata in 1895.
- George Colee died in Picolata on August 5, 1885.

However, a family *was* murdered on New River in 1836. How the story may have gotten confused could be as simple as the pronunciation of the last name. In St. Augustine, the Colees pronounce their name "COOL-ee."

5

THE TRUE AND TRAGIC STORY OF THE MURDERS AT NEW RIVER

The dawning of the New Year in 1836 was supposed to be a celebration of a hard-earned wonderful life on New River for William Cooley and his family of five. His young wife, who was believed to have been rescued from Native captivity, had birthed three healthy children—the youngest, a boy, was still in his mother's arms. The two older children, a girl and a boy, were schooled by a full-time tutor named Joseph Flinton, who was hired from Maryland and assisted by a family friend and across-the-river neighbor, Mary R. Rigby. After lessons, the children worked the family's crops with slaves and several Natives, supplying their mother's well-appointed kitchen with fresh vegetables for family meals. Their one-thousand-square-foot home, which was quite large for pioneers in those days, was always open for guests, often including the Seminoles with whom they traded goods and stories.

In mid-1835, one of their guests was Edwind T. Jenckes, "a four-hundred-pound giant from St. Augustine," wrote Kirk. It is unknown why Jenckes visited, but he is said to have also camped with the Natives for some time at the headwaters of New River.[69] He would later have important news for Cooley.

And so it was that the Christmas and New Year holiday period, two weeks off from work for festivities with family and friends, was shaping up to be the best ever, culminating on Sunday, January 5, 1836, with the Cooleys hosting their New River neighbors for a feast and a toast to the new year. It was an early evening, as they were going back to work the next day. As the guests

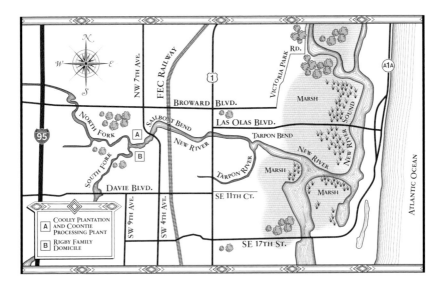

The homes of William Cooley and his across-the-river neighbors, the Rigbys, with today's major streets and railway added for reference. *Illustration by Terri Bailey, base map courtesy of the Dolph Map Company.*

departed, Mrs. Rigby and her children stayed the night to help Mrs. Cooley with the next day's clean up.[70]

The New River men were up and out early that Monday morning, boarding Cooley's wrecking boat and making their way about ten miles north to salvage the Spanish brigantine *Gil Blas*, which had been shipwrecked since September near Hillsboro Inlet by a violent hurricane. Such a large endeavor required many strong hands, hence Cooley's recruitment of most of the men in the settlement, leaving their families at home.

Unbeknownst to Cooley's salvage crew, two weeks earlier and some two hundred miles northwest, U.S. Army major Francis L. Dade was leading two companies of over one hundred men, marching through the wilderness from Tampa to Fort King, near Ocala. Moving "at the pace of the oxen drawing his six-pound cannon" and entirely without warning, gunfire erupted from all sides. Major Dade fell dead from his horse, shot through the head. About half his one hundred men also fell from the initial volley, then the Natives swarmed from the trees, knives and tomahawks in hand, killing and scalping all they encountered. Only three soldiers survived, fleeing to Fort King; one died after arriving. The Second Seminole War had begun.[71]

THE WAR WAS A continuation of the battles fought in the First Seminole War (1817–1818), and they were fought again in the Third Seminole War (1855–1858). The Indian Wars, as they are collectively called, are chronicled in many excellent books—some of which are noted in the bibliography. Suffice it to say, they were all predicated on White U.S. citizens' desire for more land in the fertile Florida territory and, perhaps more significantly in the antebellum period, an end to the Natives sheltering runaway slaves from the states to the north. Several "treaties" were forced on the Natives; the most recent, in 1832, was the Treaty of Payne's Landing, which said that the Natives had "voluntarily" agreed to emigrate peacefully to west of the Mississippi.

Only a few of the chiefs who were coerced to sign the treaty actually did so. One of those who refused was a young brave whose name became legendary as a brilliant, natural leader: Osceola. He first became known to the White man at a meeting where U.S. General Wiley Thompson swore that, unless the chiefs signed the treaty agreeing to emigrate, "they would be driven out by force." When Osceola's name was called to come forward and sign, Marjory Stoneman Douglas wrote that he proudly walked up to the table and said, "This land is ours." He then drew his knife and, "in one lightning gesture," stabbed it through the document into the table. "That is the way I sign."[72] War was inevitable.

Coinciding with the anger among the Natives about the Payne's Landing treaty was an unrelated but equally divisive incident that involved newly arrived Creeks from Alabama. The Natives who became known as Seminoles were originally part of the Creek tribes; they split off, in part, due to intertribal warfare. Over the years, the animosity had faded in no small part because of their mutual adversaries—the White men. The newly arrived Creeks evidently meshed well in the Everglades with their Seminole hosts—not so much with some of the local White population. Sometime before the summer of 1835, during a dispute with the Creeks, "swaggering white men had killed their old Chief 'Alibama' and burnt his hut," wrote Cooper Kirk. The Natives brought their complaint forward and identified the perpetrators to justice of the peace William Cooley, who took the alleged offenders into custody to be tried by the Monroe County Court in Key West. But instead of justice for the Natives, the charges were dropped by the court "due to insufficient evidence." The Creeks and some Seminoles blamed Cooley, saying, without proof, that he had withheld evidence that was essential for conviction.

Then, in the summer of 1835, Cooley's large friend Edwind Jenckes, who had been camping with the Seminoles and Creeks on the edge of the Everglades, told Cooley that the Natives' animosity toward White men, and Cooley in particular, was growing. The Natives seemed "sulky and dangerous." Later that year, their sulkiness turned to action when they began moving their women, children, and aged away from New River to camps deeper in the Everglades. Cooley reported this information to the authorities, but believing it was related to the deteriorating state of affairs between the U.S. government and the Natives over forced relocation, he evidently didn't consider the Natives' mood to be a threat to himself or the New River settlement. But, unbeknownst to Cooley, by Christmas, the "sulking" Natives had returned in secret to the New River area, bringing with them additional warriors who were prepared for battle.[73]

WORD OF THE NEW war with the Natives had not reached Cooley's salvage crew, who were hard at work freeing the *Gil Blas* from the reef near Hillsboro Inlet. Nor had it reached the New River settlement, where Mrs. Rigby and her children had finished helping Mrs. Cooley clean up from the previous night's party before returning home. With the men away, the settlement was quiet, relaxed.

Cooper Kirk's words relay the horror of what happened next:

> *Entirely without warning, a watchful band of Indian Warriors moved into the almost deserted New River Settlement during the noon hour to begin their ghastly work of revenge against the Cooley family for imagined wrongs. They waited until the Rigbys had crossed the river to their home before beginning their assault. None of the intended victims noticed the highly painted Indians as they slipped cautiously from the brush toward the Cooley home. Wholly unsuspicious of approaching danger, tutor Joseph Flinton presided as the two older children recited their assigned lessons to him, and Mrs. Cooley busied herself by attending to the needs of the infant.*
>
> *Startled by the blood-curdling war whoops, Flinton attempted to bar the door as the 15 to 20 Indians forced it with their bodies. Overcoming his resistance, the Indians horribly mangled his body even as they scalped him with an ax, while the screaming Cooley mother and children watched, momentarily stunned. Jolted into action by the macabre scene being enacted*

before their eyes, Mrs. Cooley grabbed the infant boy and pushed the other children before her. Screaming as they fled, they attempted to escape to the river. Taking careful aim, the Indians shot Mrs. Cooley about 150 yards from her house. The ball entered between her shoulders, passed through her breast and broke the arm of the infant cradled in her arms before it passed into his body. Cooley's nine-year-old son fell, a victim of a fractured skull and arm probably inflicted by a piece of firewood. Near him lay the book from which he had been reciting. The eleven-year-old girl perished with her recitation book in her hand.

Aroused by the Cooley's screaming from across the river, young William Rigby ran down to the river and witnessed the last stages of the horror. Gathering his aged widowed mother and two younger sisters, and not attempting to take one item from their own home, young Rigby and family fled southward by land and boat to seek safety in the Cape Florida Lighthouse. As they sped in fear for their lives, their clothes were torn from their bodies and their feet were horribly cut and bruised by saw grass and sharp stones. Along the way, they warned the settlers at Arch Creek and

Cape Florida Lighthouse in the 1800s. It is still standing today at Bill Baggs Cape Florida State Park on the southern tip of Key Biscayne. *Courtesy of the State Archives of Florida.*

Miami River of the terrible danger that faced them and urged them to flee to the lighthouse. The Rigbys spent two days at the lighthouse recuperating from their injuries before they could stand again on their own feet.

Back at the New River Settlement, the Indians plundered Cooley's property of everything of value. They carried away the $7,000 worth of cargo stored [at his home] *from the* Gil Blas *and drove before them his livestock. However, they did no harm to his coontie manufacturing plant, reserving it for their own future use. Two of Cooley's black slaves, Peter and a young black woman, also disappeared. Sated by the blood of the Cooley family, the Indians harmed none of the other New River settlers, all of whom made their way to Cape Florida.*[74]

There remains some question as to how and when Cooley and the *Gil Blas* salvors learned of the killings and fled for their own safety. Historian Kirk relied on Cooley's own words when he said that he had gone to Cape Florida Lighthouse, where he learned of the disaster from the Rigbys. The next day, January 7, Cooley returned to the desolate New River settlement, finding the bodies of his wife and children. As reported in the *Key West Inquirer* on January 23, 1836:

When he approached the peaceful home, he found the body of Joseph Flinton of Cecil County, State of Maryland, who acted as instructor to his children. His body was mangled, and he evidently had been killed with an axe. His two eldest children were found nearby, shot through the heart, one yet holding the book in her hand she had been learning, and the book of the other lay by his side. About 100 yards distant, he found the bodies of his wife and infant. She had also been shot through the head, and the small ball is supposed to have broken the infant's arm.

The house in which he kept arrowroot [an American name for coontie] *and the machinery with which he manufactured it were left uninjured. The Indians carried off about 12 barrels of provisions, 30 hogs and three horses, $480 in silver, his clothing, one keg of powder, over 200 pounds of lead and $7,000 worth of dry goods.*

By their tracks, Mr. Cooley computes the number of Indians at 20 to 30. They also carried off a negro man and woman and a Spanish man named Emmanuel. Our bereaved friend and neighbor caused the bodies of his loved ones decently interred as circumstances would permit, and he returned to the lighthouse on the 10th*.*[75]

At the lighthouse, Cooley encountered his slave, Peter, who had somehow escaped. Peter said that he overheard the Natives expressing rage for Cooley's failure to obtain the conviction of Chief Alibama's murderers and that this was their revenge. "Peter's disclosure of the slayers' identities confirmed Cooley's suspicions," wrote Kirk. "Indeed, they were Indians who often supped at his table as they made merry with his family."[76]

As word of the killings spread, coupled with learning of the new war with the Natives, panicked residents of south Florida abandoned their homes, fleeing to the lighthouse on Key Biscayne about thirty-miles south, tired and trail-beaten with only the clothes on their backs. Because of his position as justice of the peace and his natural leadership skills, Cooley took charge of the motley and fearful band of refugees. Taking stock of their situation at the lighthouse and realizing they were woefully inadequate, Cooley loaded settlers and slaves aboard his large schooner and, joined by other craft, set sail for the safety of Indian Key about sixty miles southwest. There, security had been significantly increased, including the formation of a militia of about fifty able-bodied islanders and seamen who quickly began fortifying the island. Immediately after disembarking, the refugees and Cooley conferred with the local militia, then he turned his sturdy schooner back into the heavy seas, back to the *Gil Blas*, and returned to Indian Key with two brass cannons and ample balls commandeered from the wreck. With those substantial armaments, the growing colony at Indian Key felt they were safe from Native attack.

It would be reasonable to assume that after finding his family gruesomely murdered, losing $12,000 in property, and assuming leadership responsibility for an untold number of south Florida refugees, William Cooley would have simply relaxed at the fortified Indian Key and waited for the war to end to resume his life. But that was not William Cooley. "For the next year and a half, official duties and private undertakings" took him from Key West to military camps near Jacksonville, west to the Suwannee River, south along the Gulf of Mexico, and back to the Keys. "A whirlwind of activities threw him into almost every conceivable situation in a territory largely unknown and unexplored by Americans," wrote Kirk. "That he survived through it all is astonishing enough; that he enhanced his reputation and sphere of influence simultaneously is almost miraculous."[77] It is also miraculous that he had no desire for revenge against the Natives, maintaining his respect, and while considering all they had taken from him, perhaps remembering all that had been taken from them.

In 1837, Cooley relocated to the west coast, in the vicinity of Tampa, to the headquarters for military operations in the territory. There, he served as a scout and express rider for the U.S. Army and Navy; he later remarried and moved to Homosassa, where he began a new chapter in his amazing life.[78]

Back at New River, the pioneer settlement was abandoned and largely remained that way for decades. The deceased Mrs. Cooley, the couple's three young children, and their faithful tutor remained buried on the riverfront where they fell, overlooking "the calm New River, the scene of bygone life and merriment," Kirk wrote. "Their tragic and senseless murder ended the New River Settlement, as first the Indians and then the United States Army took control."[79]

6
THE FORTS OF LAUDERDALE

It was mere coincidence, not connection, that the Cooley family killings happened just two weeks after the first blood was shed in the Second Seminole War. The twenty to thirty Natives who carried out the horrible attack had their own very specific grievance, valid or not, against William Cooley. His was the only family ambushed by Natives on that fateful day in January 1836. Although terrified enough to flee their homes, which they built with sweat and grit, with only the clothes on their back, not a single other New River settler was harmed. The Natives did not chase them to the Cape Florida Lighthouse or attempt to follow them to Indian Key. Their grievance was settled.

It took two years for the war to make its way down the southeast Florida coast. Also making its way south in January 1838 was a battalion of five hundred Tennessee Volunteers under the leadership of Major William Lauderdale. Lauderdale was a friend of President Andrew Jackson, alongside whom he fiercely fought in prior battles with Native Americans. Retired from the army for two decades and living a comfortable life on his successful Tennessee plantation, Lauderdale was called out of retirement by his old military mentor. The war against the Seminoles, which was waged during Jackson's presidency, was entering its third year, and the U.S. Army had little to show for it. The commander of the Florida war, Major General Thomas Jesup, was appointed by Jackson with direct orders: win the war and remove all Natives. Despite Jesup's tenacity and what

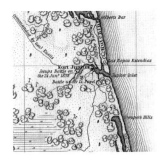

Section of the *Map of the Seat of War in Florida*, a U.S. Army map from 1838 that shows location of the Second Battle of Loxahatchee, which took place in today's Riverbend Park in Jupiter. *Courtesy of the Historical Society of Palm Beach County.*

some would call ruthless tactics (for example, he captured Seminole leaders Osceola and Micanopy by having his troops approach them under a false flag of truce), the Natives' hide-and-seek battle plan was winning. Frustrated, General Jesup called on Jackson for advice. The old warrior replied, "I know of but one man…who can and will beat the whole Indian force in Florida, [William Lauderdale]."[80] Recruited by the former president, Lauderdale then recruited five companies of volunteers, and his battalion began the five-hundred-mile trek from Tennessee to meet Jesup at the Loxahatchee River in Jupiter.

On their arrival, Jesup commissioned Lauderdale's troops as the Tennessee Mounted Infantry, and on January 24, 1838, he assigned them to the left flank of his battle line to rout Chief Sam Jones (Abaika) and his Seminole warriors from their refuge west of the Jupiter Inlet. Known as the Second Battle of the Loxahatchee (the first, having taken place two weeks earlier, was a decisive victory for the Seminoles), Jesup brought 1,500 troops against an estimated 100 to 300 Seminoles. It was a U.S. victory, although Sam Jones escaped along with a number of warriors heading south for hideaways deep in the Everglades. Significantly, that battle was the last organized resistance of the Natives during the Second Seminole War. From then on, they resorted to guerrilla warfare.[81]

General Jesup then ordered Major Lauderdale to muster his volunteers and pursue Sam Jones and his warriors south; they were accompanied by a platoon of U.S. Army regulars under the command of Lieutenant Robert Anderson. Leading the Tennesseans and a unit of "construction pioneers," Lauderdale followed the high coastal ridge that extended from Jupiter to New River, carving as they went a sixty-three-mile-long path through the untamed wilderness.[82] That is the approximate path of today's "Military Trail" from Jupiter to Fort Lauderdale.

They arrived at New River on March 5, 1838, about "one-eighth mile above Cooley's patch," presumably referring to William Cooley's homestead, the killing field of his family. There, on the north bank where the river forked, Lauderdale's troops built a substantial fort: a thirty-foot square blockhouse "with a double tier for firing" surrounded by a sixty-

A 1988 statue honoring Major William Lauderdale at the entrance of Pine Island Ridge, Davie. *Sculptor, Luis Montoya, image from the author's collection.*

by-fifty-foot fence with pickets that were seven feet tall and sunk one and a half feet into the ground. By order of General Jesup, the imposing structure was named Fort Lauderdale.[83]

Armaments in place, on March 22, a combined force of U.S. Army and Navy fighters, including the Tennessee Volunteers, embarked on the first assault on the Seminoles in their previously unreachable Everglades camps. Paddling their boats up New River against the strong current, they encountered a Native encampment on Pine Island, about five miles west of their fort as the crow flies. There, "the men waded waist deep in the water, carrying white flags in an effort to reach a truce," reported Philip Weidling and August Burghard in *Checkered Sunshine*. Perhaps having heard of the capture of Osceola and Micanopy under false white flags, the Natives fired, and the troops deployed, attacking the island. "As in so many other fruitless efforts to fight the Indians in their native habitat, the enemy escaped," leaving behind their boats, jewelry, coontie, and other provisions. A second expedition was launched a month later, only to find that the Seminole warriors had fled northwest toward Lake Okeechobee.[84] The frustration of fighting a wily enemy in such a daunting environment

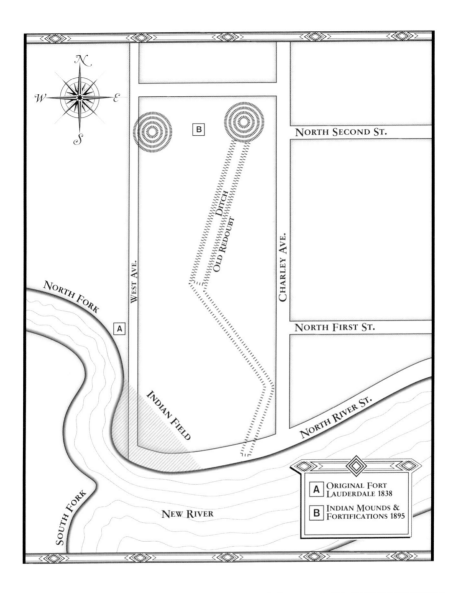

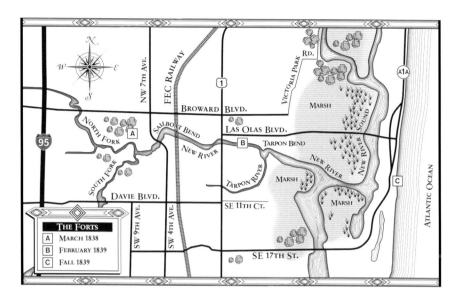

THE FORTS

A	MARCH 1838
B	FEBRUARY 1839
C	FALL 1839

Opposite, top: An interesting portion of the *1896 Town of Fort Lauderdale Plat* by A.L. Knowlton, showing "Indian Mounds," a redoubt (a defensive position generally composed of an earthen mound supplemented by felled trees, rocks, and other available material), and a ditch in which warriors could be hidden from enemy intruders. The purpose of the "Indian Field" and the history of the features is unknown. It is here that the first military Fort Lauderdale was constructed. *Illustration by Terri Bailey.*

Opposite, bottom: A sketch of the first Fort Lauderdale on the east bank of New River's north fork. *Courtesy of History Fort Lauderdale.*

Above: The approximate locations of the three military forts named for Major William Lauderdale, with today's major streets and railway added for reference. *Illustration by Terri Bailey, base map courtesy of the Dolph Map Company.*

weighed heavily on the commanders, as evidenced in a document written by General Jesup that was dated July 16, 1838:

> *If our operations have fallen short of public expectation, it should be remembered that we are attempting that which no other armies of our country had ever been required to do…not only to fight, beat and drive the enemy before us, but to go into an unexplored wilderness and catch them.*[85]

Its mission compromised, its defenders demoralized, and the logistics of maintaining, protecting, and provisioning the inland fort imposing, Fort Lauderdale was abandoned.

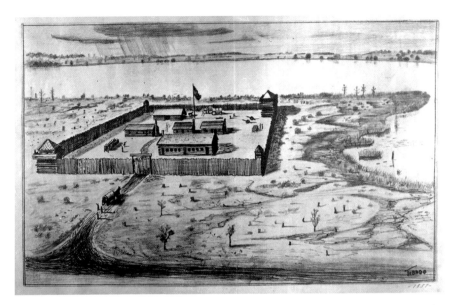

A conceptual drawing of the final Fort Lauderdale on the beach near today's Bahia Mar. It was in service from 1839 to 1842. *Courtesy of History Fort Lauderdale.*

But the area was not left unattended for long. A second fort was built farther downstream at Tarpon Bend in February 1839. The primary mission of this fort, which was also named for Lauderdale, was to be a staging area for a new fort to be built on the barrier island beach, where it could be more easily provisioned by sea.[86] In a seeming admission of the futility of fighting the Natives on their own turf, the mission of the oceanfront Fort Lauderdale was defined as a defensive one: protect shipwreck survivors from Native attacks. It is unknown whether the soldiers stationed there ever performed that service. The final fort was garrisoned continually until February 1842, near the end of the war.[87]

New River was quiet again.

LOST DECADES

When the last of the soldiers packed their bedrolls in 1842 and left their oceanfront military Fort Lauderdale, bound for parts unknown, the Seminoles were likely the only remaining inhabitants of the New River area—at least for a time. While hunting and fishing for food, they probably camped in houses that had been abandoned by terrified, fleeing White families after the Cooley murders. It is also likely that the Natives resumed processing coontie at Cooley's water-powered plant, which was carefully preserved as his home and other structures were looted and burned. Given William Cooley's proclivity to include Natives in all manners of his life (as noted earlier, they often worked his fields alongside his children and slaves and partook in his family's meals), he probably taught some of them how to run the plant. It is unlikely, though, that Cooley's brisk commercial coontie business returned; the White traders would have been reluctant to enter "hostile territory." The Seminoles were probably content to extract the coontie starch for the nourishment of their own people.

It was assumed by most early historians that, after the Cooley killings, the New River area was bereft of White settlers and remained so for decades. That assumption was challenged in a *Broward Legacy* article by Joe Knetsch, the author of over two hundred articles and eleven books on Florida's history. "There has always been a lingering doubt on the part of some researchers about the complete abandonment of the lovely New River area after the Second Seminole War, which ended in 1842." He cited papers relating to the "Indian Scare of 1849," in which small numbers of settlers scattered throughout southeast Florida, including some who were said to be from the New River area, reported increased Native activity. The settlers were frightened, so much that so they abandoned their homes and farms and "banded themselves together at Jupiter, New River, and Cape Florida for defense," while demanding that the federal government forcibly remove the feared Natives.

The army sent a squad of soldiers from Key West to investigate as far north as New River but found no signs of Natives, leaving the lieutenant in command to later report that the settlers' "fears of an outbreak among the Indians were far more imaginary than real," wrote Knetsch. After seeing to it that the settlers were safely back to their homes, the army squad returned to Key West.

While the soldiers had found no Native activity along the southeast coast, there were skirmishes around the Indian River (about 150 miles to the north) and Payne's Creek in central Florida. Seeking to deescalate the situation, the Indian Bureau asked Chief Billy Bowlegs, Sam Jones, and other Native leaders to deliver the perpetrators for justice. "Of the five braves arrested by order of Bowlegs…three were turned over, one escaped and the other was slain in an escape attempt (his severed hand was delivered as proof)."[88] The Seminoles' cooperation led the federal government to deny the settlers' demand to remove the Natives—at least at that time.

In hindsight, it is almost illogical to believe that for decades there were no White settlers in the lush New River area, prolific as it was with game and fish and rich in soil for cultivation. Add to those attributes the Armed Occupation Act of 1842, which was designed to populate vacant areas of Florida and create "an armed buffer area between the Indians and the whites." The government offered 160 acres to any head of a family or single man over eighteen who was able to carry a gun. Recipients were required to live on the land in a habitable house for five years and cultivate at least five acres. Knetsch's article listed the names of several people who received the grants, noting that they were few and far between.[89] They probably did not form much of an "armed buffer" against the perceived threat of Natives.

Statehood came to Florida in 1845, but nothing much changed. While there may have been some homes and farms around New River, anything resembling progress was paused for at least three decades.

The Third Seminole War (1855–1858), which was generally fought in central and southwest Florida, likewise did not have much effect on the New River area. Historian Joe Knetsch called the final war one of the more contrived affairs in the history of White–Native American relationships, claiming, "This war was forced upon the Native Americans in no uncertain terms." The Seminoles numbered fewer than two hundred warriors, while the U.S. Army and the Florida Militia numbered nearly two thousand men. The U.S. Army had a search-and-destroy mission with the final objective of capturing and, if possible, removing.[90] No soldiers were stationed in New River, and no battles were fought. Failing again to forcibly rid Florida of its Natives, the federal government once again attempted to bribe them. Tired after too many years of war, Billy Bowlegs accepted the government's offer and, with most of his band, sailed from Tampa to the reservations in the Midwest. After their departure, it was estimated that about one hundred Natives remained in Florida.

Then came the Civil War. When Florida formally seceded from the Union and joined the Confederacy in early 1861, "there were probably fewer than 150 settlers in the entire southeast portion of the state, an area of 6,000 square miles," wrote Colonel James C. Staubach, a Miami native and retired U.S. Army officer who had worked in the Military History Division of the National Archives. The area that would become Greater Miami "reported only 28 settlers [lived there at the time], but 40 is a more realistic estimate."[91] The greatest immediate effect of the war on south Florida may have been a minor population boom when draft dodgers and Union sympathizers fled to the isolated area after the Confederate Conscription Act was signed in 1862. Most hid on the west coast between Charlotte Harbor and Lake Okeechobee, but a few (including draft evaders and their families) probably made it to Biscayne Bay, where a semblance of support could be found.

Key West, which was, at the time, the state's second-largest town (following Pensacola) and a major shipping hub, remained in Union hands throughout the war, as did Fort Zachery Taylor on the island's southern tip and Fort Jefferson in the Dry Tortugas. From those strongholds, the Union navy placed a very effective blockade around most of Florida's coasts, further isolating the region.

Like the Indian Wars that preceded it, the Civil War's primary effect on south Florida was to thwart its progress. Isolated by near-impassable wilderness and sealed off from the sea, the forty or so residents around Biscayne Bay endured the blockade and intrusions by Union soldiers with relative calm.

The Civil War effectively ended when General Robert E. Lee surrendered his Army of Northern Virginia, the largest of the Confederacy, on April 9, 1865. Change was immediate and chaotic in Florida's capital, Tallahassee. Days before the surrender, when the war's outcome was certain, Governor

John Milton was found dead by a gunshot wound to his head—an apparent suicide. He had warned his legislature that death was preferable to rejoining the Union. Abraham K. Allison, the president of the Florida Senate, was appointed as acting governor. He served only seven weeks. The federal government officially took control of Florida on July 13, 1865, appointing former U.S. attorney William Marvin, who had been provost marshal of Key West, to the governorship. Again, this position was temporary. A statewide election was held in November. Its only candidate, Democrat David S. Walker, a Kentucky native, was elected as the eighth governor of Florida, and, with his lieutenant governor, William H. Gleason, a banker and real estate developer from New York, he commanded the state through the early Reconstruction era, from 1866 to 1868.

Abraham Lincoln was to have been the national champion of Reconstruction. Two years before war's end, the confident president created a simple and humane plan to readmit the southern states to the Union, but his assassination five days after Lee's surrender turned the matter upside down. A modified—some would say "cruel"—Reconstruction occurred under Lincoln's successor, Andrew Johnson. The former Confederate states, Florida included, were not at all ready for the dramatic changes it would bring.

"There was no economy," wrote Jerrell H. Shofner in *The New History of Florida*. "Money and credit had disappeared with the fall of the Confederacy. The means of production had ended with the abolition of slavery. There were no markets and little transportation."[92] Into this vacuum came "help" from the North, often in the form of "carpetbaggers" who were seeking opportunity in chaos. "Radical Republican representatives...came to Florida to form secret Black societies and to organize Black voters, who had suffrage (the right to vote) by congressional mandate," wrote Michael Gannon. "Their success was manifest in the results of the 1868 elections," when dozens of White southern conservative Democrats who had controlled the legislature for decades were ousted by Republicans, many of them carpetbaggers.[93]

The overhaul of the government wasn't the only upheaval in the post–Civil War South. Most of Florida's homes and institutions were still standing, and most of its families were still relatively intact, but this was not so for its neighboring Rebel states. With their destruction came desire for new beginnings, and for many in the Southeast, those new beginnings were sought farther south. A few of the more adventurous found their way to New River.

John J. "Pig" Brown, his wife, Lavinia, and their six children, aged thirteen to twenty-three, moved to New River from Georgia by way of Volusia County sometime prior to 1870. They established a hog farm on the barrier island between the Atlantic Ocean and New River Sound. It is unknown whether Pig got his nickname before or after moving to New River, and what is known about his earlier life is unremarkable. Pig's story became public when he changed his occupation from pigs to politics. In a 2009 article in *Broward Legacy*, Christopher R. Eck, a former administrator and historic preservation officer for the Broward County Historical Commission, told how Pig Brown became the first elected official in today's Broward County and how his subsequent disappearance became a tantalizing mystery.

In 1872, there were only ninety-nine registered voters in Florida's 21st State Senate District, which was composed of Dade County (which, at the time, stretched from Biscayne Bay to the Hillsboro Inlet) and its northern neighbor, Brevard County. That year, Brown ran for a seat in the legislature against "the powerful and corrupt William H. Gleason," the former Florida lieutenant governor under David Walker and, according to Eck, "an audacious carpetbagger that manipulated local government, business and community life in Dade County for a decade." Brown beat Gleason sixteen votes to fourteen, but after the votes were counted, three of Brown's votes were tossed "through underhanded manipulation," sending Gleason to Tallahassee for the 1873 legislative session. Undaunted, in 1876, Brown again ran against Gleason, and despite more election shenanigans, Brown was elected and sworn into office on February 1, 1877. It was after his single, contentious three-year legislative term that the mystery began.[94] Pig Brown and his family never returned to their New River farm.

By 1880, the New River area had grown in population, and there was widespread concern that something untoward may have happened to the popular legislator who had defeated such a powerful carpetbagger and, more importantly, triggered the beginning of the end of carpetbagger politics in the state. Conspiracy theories abounded, but without evidence, the disappearance of Pig Brown was eventually filed away, unsolved.

Over one hundred years later, Christopher Eck finally solved the mystery. In his role as a county historian, he dusted off the file and, using twenty-first-century research tools, discovered that Pig Brown, who was then a widower, spent his final years living with his son around Chokoloskee in the remote Ten Thousand Islands on Florida's west coast. It turned out the story was less a mystery than the desire of a worn-down crusading politician and pig farmer wanting to get away from it all.

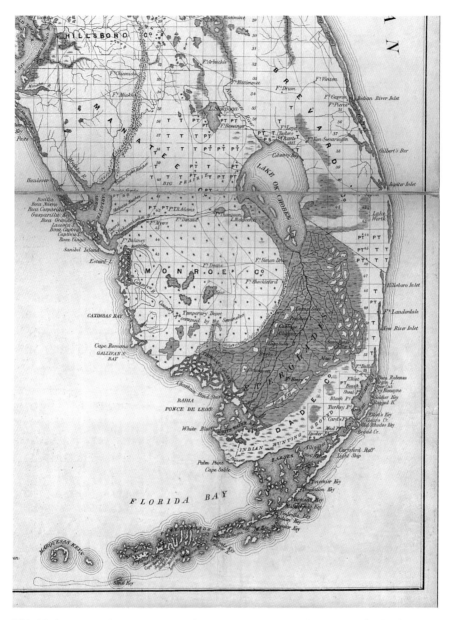

This 1859 map showing the progress of government surveys delineates the dividing line between Dade and Brevard Counties, which ran diagonally from the vicinity of Hillsboro Inlet to the lower eastern shore of Lake Okeechobee. *Courtesy of the Library of Congress.*

WASHINGTON JENKINS WAS ANOTHER pioneer who brought new life to the New River area. Known to friends and family as "Wash," the twenty-five-year-old man and his family came to south Florida in 1876 from South Carolina, originally intending to farm the rich riverfront land. In September of the same year, the United States government needed someone to man the new House of Refuge, which had been built on the beach about four miles north of the New River Inlet. Wash took the job.

Officially known as U.S. Life-Saving Station No. 4, the House of Refuge was one of five authorized by Congress between St. Augustine and Miami. The keepers, as they were known, lived full time in the sturdy, government-built and provisioned oceanfront houses for free with an annual stipend of $400. This was an attractive package considering the hardscrabble alternatives. Most keepers were listed as farmers in prior census records. Professional boating experience was not a prerequisite, as the keepers were not expected to actually save people from sinking ships. Their primary mission was to maintain a safe and well-stocked refuge for the shipwreck survivors the keepers found when walking the beach after bad storms. After being helped back to the house, the castaways were given food, water, and a safe, dry place to sleep until they could make their way home.

Wash, his wife, Mary, and their four children were comfortable at the House of Refuge. It was a "frame construction, one-story with loft, three main rooms downstairs surrounded by an eight-foot-wide veranda on three sides," explained Ruth Landini in *Broward Legacy*. A narrow kitchen with a brick chimney stove was on the north side; the windows had screens and shutters but no glass. "The keeper and his family lived downstairs…the loft, with a small window on each end, was equipped with approximately 20 cots for castaways or visitors." A boathouse with a lifeboat and large, elevated water cistern rounded out the small complex. Each station cost about $3,000 to build.[95] To replenish supplies and break the boredom of the solitary life, Wash, sometimes in the company of his family, made occasional trips to Biscayne Bay.

Wash left the lifesaving service due to ill health on January 2, 1883. After treatment at Biscayne Bay, he said he was poisoned "by one that wanted to get him out of the way," perhaps referring to his replacement as the keeper of U.S. Life-Saving Station No. 4, Edwin R. Bradley. Apparently, nothing came from that claim. Then, soon after the Bradleys moved into the house, their ten-year-old daughter died from a mysterious illness, "the same malady

Right: "Wash" Jenkins with his first wife and family. They had comfortable, if generally isolated, lives as the keepers of House of Refuge No. 4, which was located on the ocean beach about four miles north of the then-location of the New River Inlet. The house operated from 1876 to 1914, after which it became U.S. Coast Guard Station No. 6. *Courtesy of History Fort Lauderdale.*

Below: House of Refuge No. 4. Photograph taken from the ocean waterline. *Courtesy of History Fort Lauderdale.*

which had afflicted keeper Jenkins."[96] Again, no further documentation has been found of this illness, but it could be assumed that contaminated food or water may have been to blame for both of the individuals' illnesses.

New River's lonely isolation was coming to an end. In 1870, the state commissioned Marcellus Williams to produce a detailed survey of south Florida—the first since a rough sketch was made in 1845. An accurate survey opened the door for future homeowners and speculators with means and ambition to see beyond the wilderness to the cities of the future. The settlements around Lake Worth and Biscayne Bay were growing, and New River was on the path between the two.

PATH OF PROGRESS

After more than four decades of despondency, south Florida, New River in particular, needed some good news. It came from an unlikely source.

Dr. James A. Henshall was a colorful Kentucky physician, outdoorsman, and naturalist. In 1884, he published *Camping and Cruising in Florida*, which, in retrospect, was a chamber of commerce–worthy book about what he had christened "the land of the perpetual summer." In it, he described, in delightful detail, the voyages he had made in 1879 and 1882 as a remedy for what he called the "fickle climate and too generous and imprudent mode of living common to Central Kentucky."

Accompanying him on the first excursion were five patients with a variety of ailments and his setter puppy, Gipsy Queen.[97] After arriving in Jacksonville following a three-day journey from Kentucky on a variety of conveyances, and against the advice of a friend who tried to dissuade him from leaving civilized northeast Florida (he said they "would be devoured by fleas, sandflies, and mosquitoes"), the determined doctor and his sickly crew set sail south aboard his chartered boat, *Blue Wing*, to find a healing climate and healthy sport.

After several enjoyable stops along Florida's upper east coast, they made their way south to the New River Inlet, entering the sound and proceeding north a couple of miles to the boat landing for House of Refuge No. 4, which was still being kept by Wash Jenkins at the time. Welcoming company to his lonely refuge, Jenkins gladly served as their guide to the wonders of the untamed land and water, which was abundant with game and fish.

THE BLUE WING OFF JUPITER LIGHT.

The *Blue Wing* off the coast of the Jupiter Lighthouse. *Image from* Camping & Cruising in Florida *by James Alexander Henshall, 1884.*

"New River is a fine stream," Henshall wrote. "At its mouth, crevallé are taken with grains to the weight of thirty or forty pounds each, which are smoked and dried and are superior in flavor to smoked halibut." The group met a Native who was on his way upstream in search of egret plumes; he graciously allowed the White men to examine his rifle, powder horn, and knife but declined their offer to buy his buckskin moccasins and leggings. Their curiosity about the Seminoles, fueled in part by the incendiary stories about them in newspapers during the Indian Wars, led the doctor and his crew to carry out an excursion upstream to Pine Island on the edge of the Everglades in a borrowed sailboat-canoe. It was there that the only local battle of the Second Seminole War took place. The curious explorers found equally curious, nonthreatening Seminoles and "conversed with them in broken English," which evolved into a two-day visit with chiefs Little Tommy and Little Tiger and their tribe.[98]

With their exploration of New River fulfilled, the doctor and his crew sailed south to Biscayne Bay, where they explored, hunted, and fished on the outskirts of the Everglades before returning to Jacksonville. Their four-month excursion ended in May 1879. Returning home to Kentucky, the doctor's crew was no longer sickly—each retained the healthy weight they had gained in south Florida.

Two years later, Dr. Henshall was ready for a return trip, this time with his wife, whose health was failing. He was hoping to "restore the bloom to her cheeks, brightness to her eyes, and vigor to her body." Departing Jacksonville just before Christmas 1881 and chartering the schooner *Rambler* and her skipper along the way, the couple arrived at New River a few weeks later and reconnected with their friend and guide Wash Jenkins. There, Henshall wrote a vivid description:

> *New River, for six miles above its mouth, is the straightest, deepest, and finest river I have seen in Florida, although a narrow one. It is famous for its sharks (regular man-eaters, some of them) and for the immense number and variety of its fishes....Rushing in and out with the tide...fishes can be seen by the thousands, which snap at anything, even a bit of rag tied to the hook and thrown to them by a strong hand line.*[99]

They spent two or three days at New River, "shooting ducks, coots, and snipe, and one day went out with [Wash] Jenkins and his dogs for deer." While waiting and watching, Dr. Henshall spotted some quail and began to whistle to call them. Soon, about thirty were all around him, hopping over his feet, "cocking up their cunning little heads and looking knowingly at [him] with their bright round eyes."

The couple's cruise continued south to Biscayne Bay—a side trip to the Everglades—then around Key West into the Gulf of Mexico for exploration of the west coast. Henshall's wife's health improved, and their journey aboard the *Rambler* ended, chronicled for the world to read:

> *Farewell, Florida!*
> *Thy stately palms and whisp'ring pines,*
> *Thy silent cypress, clamb'ring vines,*
> *Thy orange groves and flowers rare,*
> *Thy spicy shrubs and scented air,*
> *Farewell!*
>
> *Farewell, Florida!*
> *Thy Everglades, savannas green,*
> *Thy crystal streams and lakes serene,*
> *Thy coral reefs, thy sunny keys,*
> *Thy mangrove isles, thy summer breeze,*
> *Farewell!*

Farewell, Florida!
Thy starry nights, thy balmy days,
Thy azure skies, thy sun's bright rays,
Thy ocean blue, thy land-locked bays,
Thy silver sheen, thy golden haze.
Farewell![100]

Dr. Henshall, in reporting the successful medical outcomes of his therapeutic excursions to Florida, added that some of his patients considered returning there to live. They were certainly not alone.

Jacksonville, St. Augustine, and the other well-established towns in the northern half of the state had long enjoyed the company of people we call "tourists" today. Many came for medicinal reasons, others to escape frozen winters; still more sought riches in the new frontier. Among those seeking both warmth and riches was William Brickell, who bypassed north Florida for the new frontier and abounding opportunities on the southeast coast.

An active life preceded Brickell's Florida quest. Born and raised in Ohio, he became a California gold rush "forty-niner" in his younger years and then followed the gold to Australia, where he established a successful mining tools and supplies business and built and operated a luxury hotel. In 1862, he married Mary Bulmer. The next day, the newlyweds sailed for America and eventually settled in Cleveland, where Brickell dabbled in the oil and real estate businesses. While in Cleveland, William and Mary had a passing relationship with a man "who would play a much larger role in their lives three decades later," according to Beth Brickell, the unrelated author of *William and Mary Brickell*. The Brickells lived about five blocks away from Henry M. Flagler, Beth Brickell wrote, and would have attended the same Presbyterian church as the wealthy industrialist. Mary Brickell was said to have seen Flagler "almost daily" when they lived in Cleveland.[101] In 1867, Flagler's across-the-street neighbor, John D. Rockefeller, invited Flagler to join him and Samuel Andrews in their oil business, which they named after themselves. Three years later, they incorporated Standard Oil, which soon controlled some 90 percent of all oil production in the United States.[102]

While Rockefeller, Flagler, and Andrews prospered, the Brickells began to sour on Cleveland after facing a series of financial setbacks and bitter winters. Having grown accustomed to warmer weather in Australia, the Brickells set their sights toward the South, where they learned that some large tracts of land had become available in southeast Florida.[103] Most of the land was located around Biscayne Bay, but one 640-acre tract was located on

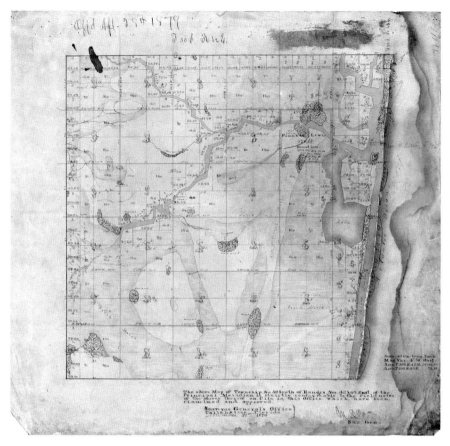

An 1870 plat map of Township 50 South, Ranges 42 and 43 East (today's Greater Fort Lauderdale). This map was made around the time that William and Mary Brickell first visited the area. *Courtesy of the State Archives of Florida.*

New River. That one square mile was the Frankee Lewis Donation, which was originally owned by New River pioneer Mrs. Frankee Lewis, who had since passed. Interested, William Brickell traveled to Florida in 1870 and was soon joined by Mary. They liked what they saw. Between 1870 and 1874, they purchased land around Biscayne Bay and, in Mary's name only, the Lewis Donation on New River. That purchase, and Mary's tenacity, set the stage for the future town of Fort Lauderdale.

By 1874, the northern border between Dade and Brevard Counties had been moved to a horizontal line running from the north shore of Lake Okeechobee to the St. Lucie Inlet, encompassing the entirety of the southeast coast of Florida. Most of the population growth was concentrated

Guy Metcalf, circa 1890.
Courtesy of the State Archives of Florida.

in the state's northern half. Everything south of Lake Worth was called South Dade, which had fewer than three hundred White inhabitants, mostly men, and about the same number of Natives. Two major decisions made by the Dade County Commission dramatically impacted South Dade County. The first was to hold a special election in 1889 to move the county seat from Miami to the more centrally located town of Juno, just north of Lake Worth, allowing greater citizen participation and easier access to the county court system and records office for filing deeds and other official documents. The commission's second decision was a commitment to build a county road from the Lake Worth area to Biscayne Bay, facilitating access to the relocated county seat. These decisions opened the door for an enterprising newspaperman and colorful pioneer named Guy Metcalf.

Originally from Ohio, Metcalf settled in Melbourne, where his father was a lawyer and owner of a lumber company. There, in 1887, he founded the *Indian River News*. When the county seat moved to Juno two years later, his newspaper followed under a new name, the *Tropical Sun*. But Metcalf wasn't content just being the publisher of Dade County's first newspaper. While retaining the paper and the influence it afforded, he recast himself as a road builder. His low bid of $24.50 a mile earned him the contract to build the new county road. In actuality, it was less a "road" than an eight-foot-wide strip of dirt that was partially cleared of trees, stumps, palmettos, and rocks. "Successive trips by mules and wagons would pack down the road," explained Stuart McIver in the *Sun-Sentinel* newspaper a century later.[104]

The new road was to cross New River at Tarpon Bend, but that didn't sit well with Mary Brickell, as it would have bisected her property (the old Frankee Lewis Donation), greatly diminishing its future value. With passion, she took her complaint to the Dade County Commission in Juno. While the back-and-forth bickering between Mary Brickell and Dade County about the road's route continued, Metcalf ignored it all and began a new venture—a stagecoach line to run on the road that he was hired to build through Tarpon Bend and which was protested by Mrs. Brickell. The line was to run from the south end of Lake Worth

Stagecoach camp manager, ferry operator, Indian trader, postmaster, general store proprietor, land agent, banker, civic leader, promoter, and politician Frank Stranahan. *Courtesy of History Fort Lauderdale.*

(today's Lantana) to a new settlement called Lemon City (the northern part of today's Miami) on Biscayne Bay. The two-day trip would require overnight accommodations and a ferry crossing at the halfway point, which happened to be Mrs. Brickell's property at Tarpon Bend. Without seeking approval from Mrs. Brickell, Metcalf proceeded with plans to establish the camp and crossing on her property, recruiting his cousin, Frank Stranahan, to build and manage it. Stranahan, a former Ohio steel mill worker, was then living in Melbourne.

Stranahan wasted no time in relocating to the site of his new opportunity, arriving at Tarpon Bend in January 1893. Precisely when the camp became operational is uncertain, but in February of that year, Jacksonville's *Florida Times Union* published an article praising the trips that took place three times a week "in well-equipped, roomy, easy-riding covered stages." The article also commended the "good and comfortable lodging at New River, the finest tarpon fishing grounds in Florida. $3 per day. Round trip for $16, one way $10." The next month, Metcalf's newspaper, the *Tropical*

Sun, reported that the stagecoach was "a commodious vehicle which will seat six passengers comfortably. It has a cover and is provided with side curtains, which may be lowered when necessary to protect passengers from the sun or rain. Usually, they are rolled up so that one has an excellent opportunity of seeing the comparatively unknown country lying between Lake Worth and New River, [a distance of about thirty miles that took some thirteen hours to traverse]."[105]

Other reporters were not so kind. A retrospective first-person report in the *Dade County Directory* told of a trip north from Lemon City "on the old trap then called a hack, the motive power being mules that had not been curried since their arrival in Dade County." Commenting on their mulish demeanor, the writer said they "seemed to be at the point of lying down and going to sleep at any moment."[106]

Meanwhile, Mary Brickell, not content to let Dade County commissioners and the opportunistic Guy Metcalf decide the fate of her prized square mile of land around Tarpon Bend, took matters into her own hands. On April 13, 1893, she notified the commission, "I have had a road cut and grubbed on the section line at New River. Please have the ferry moved and use the new road within thirty days." The tenacious Mary Brickell was victorious, and the county road was rerouted to the western boundary of her property. The county road became U.S. 1, which explains why, for southbound travelers, the highway jogs west at today's Sunrise Boulevard before returning south at Federal Highway. The opposite is true for northbound travel.

Headstrong and with great foresight, Mary Brickell and her husband, William, were major landowners who, along with Julia Tuttle and others, helped shape the future of southeast Florida. *Courtesy of History Fort Lauderdale.*

Then there was the matter of the overnight camp on Mary Brickell's property at Tarpon Bend, which was getting busier every week. This time, Mrs. Brickell went directly to Frank Stranahan and offered to give him, at no charge, ten acres of land with three hundred feet of river frontage about three-quarters of a mile west of the original Tarpon Bend camp. The caveat was that he had to move the camp and ferry to his new property. Why Stranahan received the valuable gift instead of his boss, Metcalf, is a matter of speculation. Harry Kersey wrote:

> [Stranahan] *obviously bore no legal or financial responsibility in establishing the hack line's overnight camp on Brickell property. It is possible that the Brickells elected to deed the property to Stranahan rather than Metcalf because the former was willing to cooperate in moving the camp. Another possibility is that the Brickells and Stranahan reached an understanding whereby he would represent the Brickell interests on New River. He did, in fact, serve as their land agent in later years. In any case, the ten acres of property on New River…was the first Frank Stranahan acquired in what is today Broward County.*[107]

On part of his new property (the location of today's Stranahan House), Stranahan constructed a fine campsite with seven large Adirondack-style tents—two for sleeping (one for "gents" and the other for "ladies")—a kitchen, a dining area, a recreation center, storage for feed and provisions, and Stranahan's room and office, all arranged around a large campfire. On completion, Stranahan sent his cousin a letter on Metcalf's real estate company letterhead with sketches that showed the camp's location and layout.

Stranahan's good fortune of becoming a waterfront property owner at no cost did not seem to affect his patronage from Metcalf. In August 1893, the Dade County commission gave Metcalf a license to operate a ferry across New River, from the new camp on the north bank to the southern continuation of the county road he was hired to build. Metcalf gave Stranahan the responsibility to manage and operate the ferry in addition to his camp responsibilities. With the county's grant of license came rules. The ferry crossing had to provide service seven days a week from 6:00 a.m. to 9:00 p.m., with a maximum one-hour waiting time and preset charges for crossing: passengers in any vehicle (except the driver), twenty-five cents each; persons on horseback, forty cents; a two-horse wagon and driver, sixty cents; a one-horse wagon and driver, forty cents; and cattle, lead horses, and mules, twenty-five cents each.

With the "modern" stagecoach running a fairly regular schedule of trips between the southeast population centers, it was only logical that it should become the U.S. mail carrier for the area, replacing the storied "barefoot mailmen" who had carried the mail along the beaches as far back as 1869. Again, Frank Stranahan was the beneficiary, becoming the postmaster for the New River area.

While the stagecoach line and its overnight camp evolved as a welcomed and generally reliable alternative to travel by boat on the often-dangerous Atlantic Ocean, it had its limitations—hauling freight and food being the

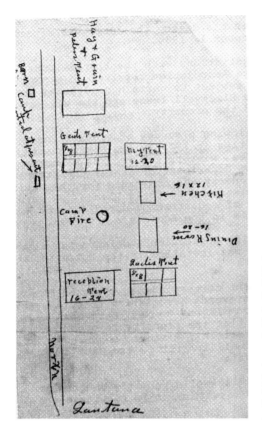

Left: Frank Stranahan was justifiably proud of the new stagecoach camp he established on his property fronting the new county road, and he sent his cousin Guy Metcalf a detailed sketch (north at the bottom of the image). *Courtesy of History Fort Lauderdale.*

Below: Crossing New River by ferry, circa 1893, at the site of today's Henry E. Kinney Tunnel (U.S. 1) which was completed in 1960. *Courtesy of History Fort Lauderdale.*

most significant. Other areas of the growing state had the advantage of rivers as their primary inland transportation corridors. The St. Johns, at 310 miles long, was the longest river contained within the state, and it connected today's Indian River County with the inlet and wharves of Jacksonville and made the growth in northeast and north-central Florida possible. No navigable river connected south Florida with the growth to the north.

What most of the east coast of Florida *did* have was an abundance of disconnected lakes, bays, sounds, and lagoons, various names for the naturally occurring bodies of water between the barrier islands and the mainland. Just after Florida became a U.S. possession in 1819, the new territorial council recommended dredging an east coast canal by connecting those bodies of water. Early efforts proved fruitless, but in 1881, four enterprising St. Augustine entrepreneurs decided to take on the challenge and incorporated the Florida Coast Line Canal and Transportation Company. Dr. John Diament Westcott, the former surveyor general of Florida, became the company's president, and James Louis Colee became the company's engineer. Westcott's son-in-law, Henry Gaillard, and James Hallowes, whose Florida lineage dated back to 1771, rounded out the company's four founding members.

"The Florida Canal Company's directors were a uniformly distinguished lot, and the venture's 74-year-old president proved no exception," wrote William Crawford in *Florida's Big Dig.* Westcott was a member of the Sons of the American Revolution and "pursued careers as a physician, surveyor, geologist, mineralogist, and chemist. He even delivered the mail in the primitive Florida wilderness." He served in the state house of representatives, was surveyor general of Florida, and was a Confederate army major during the Civil War.[108]

Colee, pronounced "COOL-ee" in his hometown St. Augustine, was the first son of George Colee, whose family was misidentified as the victims of the 1836 Native killings at New River. "Before the Civil War, James Colee owned a lumber mill and considerable land. During the conflict, Colee, like Westcott, served on the side of the Confederacy. A stockholder in the First National Bank of St. Augustine, Colee also operated the St. Augustine Transfer Company with his son, Louis."[109] The transfer company had its origins running a stagecoach line between Picolata on the St. Johns River and St. Augustine, a distance of about eighteen miles. The Colees later brought the business into town to escort wealthy visitors around the Oldest City. Colee also served as St. Johns

Left: Dr. John D. Westcott, seen here in his Confederate army major's uniform, was the surveyor general of Florida before he became the president of the Florida Coast Line Canal and Transportation Company in 1881. *Courtesy of the Virginia Museum of History and Culture.*

Right: James Louis Colee was a founding shareholder and civil engineer for the canal company that opened Florida's east coast to safe inland boat traffic. He was the company's longest-serving employee and later owned substantial amounts of land in today's Palm Beach and Broward Counties. *Courtesy of the Colee family collection.*

County's state representative and a county commissioner. He became the canal company's longest-serving employee and played a role in the development of today's Fort Lauderdale, owning, for a brief period, some of the area's prime waterfront real estate.

Through its 1881 state charter, the canal company was authorized to construct the waterway and collect tolls along its route—ten cents per boat foot—by extending chains from one bank to the other at specified locations. While toll collecting apparently continued on the waterway until the 1920s, it was never enough to cover the tremendous cost of construction and maintenance—or to even pay the toll collectors. The big money was in land grants: 3,840 acres of state land was granted for each mile of waterway dredged.[110] Harry Kersey wrote that the canal company ultimately received over a million acres of land along Florida's east coast for its work.[111]

Soon after receiving its charter, the canal company began digging south of St. Augustine in the Matanzas River. "The dredging was hard," Crawford wrote. "By January 1883, only four miles of canal…had been completed." Skills, machinery, and technique quickly evolved, though, and by that summer, dredges were working reaches from the north and south and meeting in the middle. Among the reaches worked in the early 1890s was the one between the Jupiter Inlet and Lake Worth, and this was soon followed by dredges working south from Lake Worth and north from New River. "Canal construction required that workmen have their supplies shipped southward to locations along the advancing canal and that they live on the mainland work site," wrote Cooper Kirk:

> *Tarpon Bend, high, dry land, shaded by oak trees, just off New River Sound, was selected as the work camp for the reach between Lake Worth and New River. The Tarpon Bend camp was named for canal engineer James Louis Colee. Decades later, when William and Mary Brickell platted their land encompassing the camp, they named the subdivision Colee Hammock.*

A canal company dredge at work about seven miles south of the Matanzas Inlet, heading south toward Daytona. *Ernest A. Meyer photograph, courtesy of the St. Augustine Historical Society Research Library.*

Subsequent settlers, confusing the name Colee with Cooley, erroneously thought that this location was where the Cooley family had been killed by the Indians in 1836. The true location of the attack was near the forks of New River, where the military Fort Lauderdale was situated in 1838.[112]

The dredges working north and south between Lake Worth and New River met in August 1895. "The canal company placed one of its boats—the *Hittie*—on the waterway, scheduling a run between the two settlements every three weeks, spelling the demise of the old hack line," wrote Crawford.[113]

By the time the hack line completed its last bumpy ride, Frank Stranahan had moved on to bigger and better endeavors than being a stagecoach camp innkeeper. With financial backing from Morris Benson Lyman, the hack's agent in Lantana and proprietor of a successful store there, Stranahan built a single-story trading post on the waterfront of his ten-acre New River property. The sign he placed on the building read "Ft. Lauderdale," after the old military forts, thus establishing a moniker for the emerging community and becoming its defining center of activity. He developed a brisk trade with the Seminoles, whose canoes arrived from their camps in the Everglades filled with otter pelts, bird plumes, and alligator hides for sale and departed with manufactured products purchased from Stranahan's store. With customers few and far between, excess merchandise went to Lyman's store in the more-populated area around Lake Worth, utilizing spacious and reliable transportation between the two retail centers via boats on the new waterway.

By early 1896, the last leg of the southern waterway was complete, linking New River Sound with Biscayne Bay. It was the harbinger of what would become Florida's Gold Coast. Steamboats carrying goods and passengers could then travel safely between the growing population and commercial centers around Lake Worth and the relatively primitive but attractive land around Biscayne Bay, which was already being prepped for progress by enterprising entrepreneurs Julia Tuttle and William and Mary Brickell, among others.

The waterway also afforded safe passage for the luxury yachts of wealthy potential investors who were exploring the newly opened frontier. By 1898, Stranahan had extended his wharf about one hundred feet west from his trading post to accommodate the well-heeled mariners, making Fort Lauderdale a popular port of call.

While all eyes around New River were focused on the waterway, the expanding commercial enterprises of Frank Stranahan, and the Brickells'

The opening of the Florida Coast Line Canal meant larger boats could safely navigate on inland waters. The steamer *Suwanee* visited New River years later. *Courtesy of the State Archives of Florida.*

Frank Stranahan, pictured here on the porch of his trading post, created an identity for the emerging New River settlement by erecting the sign, "Ft. Lauderdale." *Courtesy of History Fort Lauderdale.*

Stranahan extended his wharf to accommodate the larger freighters and luxury yachts that were then traveling along the new Florida Coast Line Canal. New River was said to be twenty-five feet deep at the wharf and thirty feet deep in the middle. *Courtesy of History Fort Lauderdale.*

real estate activities, another man who was well known in the industrialized northern United States was about to transform Florida's east coast.

Henry Flagler had made his first trip to Florida in February 1878, accompanied by his wife, the former Mary Harkness. The hastily arranged trip was meant to give his seriously ill wife a reprieve from the bitterly cold winter of their New York City home. After a long trip by rail, which was made more arduous due to the poorly maintained railroads south of Virginia, the couple arrived in Jacksonville and stayed at the newly built St. James, the premier hotel in the state. With little to do while his wife convalesced, Flagler took an overnight excursion to St. Augustine. He was not impressed, finding the nation's oldest town backward, lacking transportation and good lodging. Flagler was so disappointed with Florida that he cut their visit short and was back in the Standard Oil boardroom by mid-March. Mary never fully recovered and died in 1881.[114]

Flagler married Ida Alice Shourds in June 1883. It was a union shrouded in mystery as to the bride's background and Flagler's motivations. Biographer Thomas Graham wrote that, while much is unknown, "it fits into what was becoming a pattern in Flagler's life: an attempt by a

middle-aged man to recapture his youth."[115]
Six months later, Flagler and his bride arrived
in St. Augustine from New York for a warm-
weather vacation of rest, relaxation, and
rejuvenation. With the opening of the new San
Marco Hotel overlooking Matanzas Bay and
the 1695 Spanish fort Castillo de San Marcos
(then known by its American name, Fort
Marion), the ancient city finally had proper
accommodations for a man of Flagler's stature.

"Flagler had come to Florida with a new
wife; he was also prepared to renew his life,"
wrote Graham, a professor emeritus of Flagler
College.[116] After seventeen years of building the
greatest trust monopoly in the history of the world
and then fighting shipping wars with railroads and
antitrust investigations from Congress, Flagler

Henry M. Flagler, the man
responsible for the awakening
of Florida's east coast. *Courtesy
of the State Archives of Florida.*

was weary. With his marriage to the younger (thirty-seven to his fifty-five) and
fiery redhead Ida Alice, Flagler was seeking not only physical and emotional
rejuvenation, but entrepreneurial rejuvenation as well.[117]

Arriving first in Jacksonville, the Flaglers made the final leg of their journey
on a recently completed railroad that linked that city with St. Augustine, a
forty-mile trip. After settling into their luxury accommodations at the San
Marco, the Flaglers did what most visitors did: they took a tour around the
ancient city in a horse-drawn carriage from Colee Stables. Proprietor Louis
Albert (L.A.) Colee, the eldest child of canal company engineer James Louis
Colee, personally conducted the tour aboard a barouche drawn by two gray
horses.[118] Flagler took particular interest in available real estate; some say it
was on that carriage tour that he decided to get into the hospitality business
and selected the five-acre site of his first hotel.

In what today would be rightly considered an amazingly fast timeline,
Flagler purchased the property and then began construction of his luxury
hotel on December 1, 1885, just ten months after he first arrived in St.
Augustine. To speed up the delivery of construction materials and workers
from the north, Flagler purchased the Jacksonville, St. Augustine and Halifax
River Railroad on the final day of 1885. That purchase marked a major
milestone in the development of Florida's entire east coast.

Just two years after his workers first put their shovels in the marshy
ground, Flagler presided over the grand opening of his 540-room Hotel

Ponce de Leon in January 1888. And what a hotel it was. An architectural and engineering marvel, the Spanish Renaissance–style hotel was one of the nation's first electrified buildings and the first major poured-in-place concrete building in the United States.

Grand as the Hotel Ponce de Leon was, Flagler's business experience taught him the value of thwarting competition by controlling as much of the environment around his enterprises as possible. For his St. Augustine venture, that meant buying the adjacent luxury hotel, Casa Monica, which was renamed Cordova by Flagler. He also built a new hotel, the Alcazar, across the street from the Ponce de Leon.

Controlling the environment also meant controlling and improving access to his properties. His purchase of the Jacksonville, St. Augustine and Halifax River Railroad was initially a construction logistics solution; however, as completion of his destinations drew near, the railroad's primary mission became the comfortable and convenient transportation of guests. But there was a problem. The railroad operated on less expensive narrow-gauge tracks, which were three feet apart as opposed to the standard four feet, eight and a half inches. Interconnections were impossible. Flagler converted the line to standard gauge and then purchased three more railroads, converting them to the U.S. standard where necessary. By 1889, Flagler's system offered Florida travelers rail connections all the way to Daytona.

Along the way, he bought and renovated the Hotel Ormand in Ormand Beach and then set his sights south. However, instead of looking for other railroads to buy, he built new ones, encouraged by a new Florida land grant law that offered eight thousand acres for every mile of new railway constructed. With that incentive (through which Flagler eventually received over two million acres), the railway charged south, reaching today's West Palm Beach on March 22, 1894.

Some have speculated that Flagler may have intended to terminate his railway there, relaxing at his Royal Poinciana Hotel, which opened the same year, and supervising construction of his winter retreat, Whitehall, a seventy-five-room, one-hundred-thousand-square-foot Palm Beach mansion designed by the same architects as his Ponce de Leon. But this was not so, according to Florida East Coast Railway historian Seth H. Bramson. "[It is] very possible that Flagler planned all along to continue the railroad, at least to Miami and possibly further south," said Bramson in *Speedway to Sunshine*. "In fact, he had already received a state charter to build the railroad all the way to Miami in 1892." Citing the tycoon's keen insightfulness into human nature, Bramson said, "It now seems extremely likely that Flagler was simply waiting for the best opportunity to extend the railroad," and he added that there was a good chance he could have received vast amounts of land in exchange.[119] Flagler's foresight proved correct.

———⚬⚬⚬———

SOMETIMES, FROM ADVERSITY COMES opportunity. A series of devasting freezes in 1894 and 1895 destroyed the central Florida orange crop, which was vital to the financial solvency of Flagler's railway. It also opened a window of opportunity for Biscayne Bay real estate investors Julia Tuttle and William and Mary Brickell. A romantic but, according to FEC historian Bramson, completely false fable said that Tuttle mailed orange blossoms to Flagler to demonstrate that south Florida groves were unaffected by the freeze, encouraging the continuation of the railway south. Instead, Bramson said, Tuttle piqued Flagler's interest by sending a wire stating that the Biscayne Bay region was unaffected by the freezes, causing Flagler to dispatch his lieutenants, James E. Ingraham and Joseph R. Parrott, south to investigate. Years later, according to Beth Brickell, Ingraham revealed his version of the orange blossom story in a speech to the Miami Woman's Club.[120] A passage in a 1986 book by David Leon Chandler recites Ingraham's story:

> *Shortly after the freeze, I came to Miami, and I found at Lauderdale, Lemon City, Buena Vista, Coconut Grove and at Cutler orange trees, lemon trees and lime trees blooming…without a leaf hurt, vegetables growing… untouched. There had been no frost there. I gathered up a lot of blooms from these various trees, put them in damp cotton, and after an interview with Mrs. Tuttle and Mr. and Mrs. Brickell…I hurried to St. Augustine, where I called on Mr. Flagler and showed him the orange blossoms.*[121]

Ingraham said he told Flagler he believed this was the only place in Florida unaffected by the freezes and that it would become the base of the citrus industry and a great shipping opportunity for his railroad. He also said that he had in his possession written offers from Tuttle and the Brickells for large tracts of land around Biscayne Bay in exchange for extending the railroad. Flagler looked at Ingraham for a few minutes in perfect silence before asking, "How soon can you arrange for me to go to Miami?"[122] The deal was done, and plans were quickly made to extend Flagler's railway south.

To get to Miami, the tracks had to go through the growing settlement of Fort Lauderdale on New River. By that time, Mary Brickell had taken over management of the family's properties and would do anything to protect her New River land investments. Flagler wanted his railroad to run the relatively straight line along the high coastal ridge, essentially the same path originally selected by Dade County commissioners for the county road. That path would have run through the middle of the Brickells' most prized property on New River, Tarpon Bend. Again, the steadfast Mary said, "no way," and refused to sell Flagler the land needed for his right of way. Consequently, the railroad tracks were bent to the west near today's Northeast 16th Street

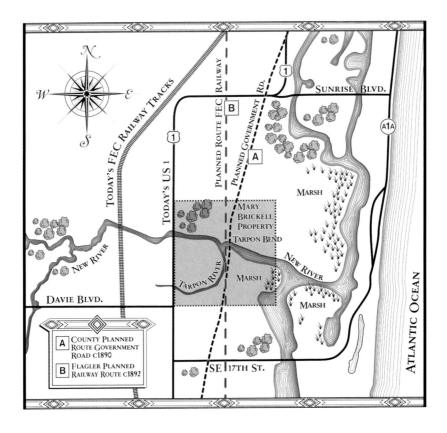

The tenacious Mary Brickell preserved her precious property by convincing Dade County to change the path of its proposed county road (today's U.S. 1). She then denied Henry Flagler the right of way needed for his railway, forcing him to curve his tracks west of today's Colee Hammock and Rio Vista. *Illustration by Terri Bailey, base map courtesy of the Dolph Map Company.*

before returning south at Sistrunk Boulevard. The tranquility of Tarpon Bend was again preserved.

Flagler hired former New Smyrna mayor and citrus grower Philemon N. Bryan to complete the construction of the railway from Cypress Creek to New River (about ten miles).[123] Unlike his grand development of St. Augustine, Ormand Beach, and Palm Beach, Flagler had no plans to make his New River stop anything more than a freight depot, believing it to be just good farming land and, therefore, a shipping opportunity. To stimulate agricultural growth beyond the small mom-and-pop farms, Bryan was also assigned by Flagler to begin large-scale farming in the area. Showing entrepreneurial ambition and a greater appreciation for the area's potential, Bryan built his wood-frame house across the street from the small train depot, using part of the home for guest lodging as the Bryan House. In 1905, when the Bryans' sons, Reed and Tom, convinced their parents to build a new family home, Philemon also commissioned a riverfront hotel, the New River Inn, which was built with concrete blocks made with beach sand to withstand Florida's notorious storms and featured hot and cold running water and gas lights.[124] The hotel and the Bryans' new home were built by Edwin T. King, and at the time of this writing, they are still standing at History Fort Lauderdale on Southwest 2nd Avenue. Reed and Tom Bryan continued their father's legacy and became pillars of the emerging town of Fort Lauderdale.

Philemon N. Bryan, one of Fort Lauderdale's founding fathers. *Courtesy of History Fort Lauderdale.*

James E. Ingraham, the president of the Florida East Coast Railway's real estate division, Model Land Company, which was established in 1896. *Courtesy of the State Archives of Florida.*

Like the Bryans, the Brickells had bigger plans than simply watching trains loaded with produce as they passed through. William and Mary had added about 895 acres to their already substantial New River holdings, and in 1895, they took a giant

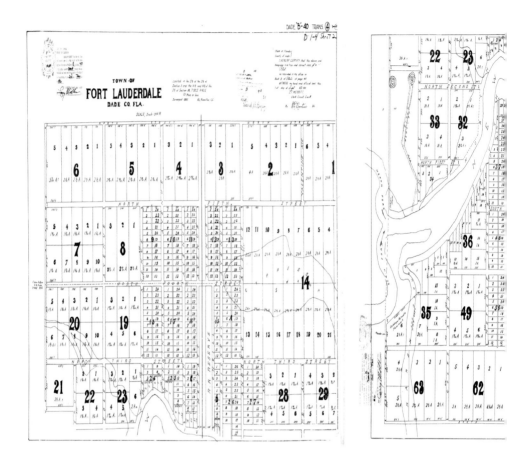

The 1896 plat, in three parts, of the town of Fort Lauderdale. Drawn by A.L. Knowlton, signed by Mary and William Brickell, and directed by the Model Land Company's James E. Ingraham. *Provided by Broward County Engineering Department.*

step forward by hiring A.L. Knowlton, a civil engineer from West Palm Beach, to plat the new town of Fort Lauderdale. While the Brickells' signatures appeared on the plat, they relinquished their land-planning decisions to Flagler's James Ingraham, who, in 1896, was appointed president of the Florida East Coast Railway's new real estate division, the Model Land Company.[125]

On February 22, 1896, the first FEC Railway train arrived at Fort Lauderdale, setting off a whirlwind of activity. By April 15, the FEC had extended the tracks to Miami; the first regularly scheduled passenger train service began running on April 22.[126] Between those giant leaps into the

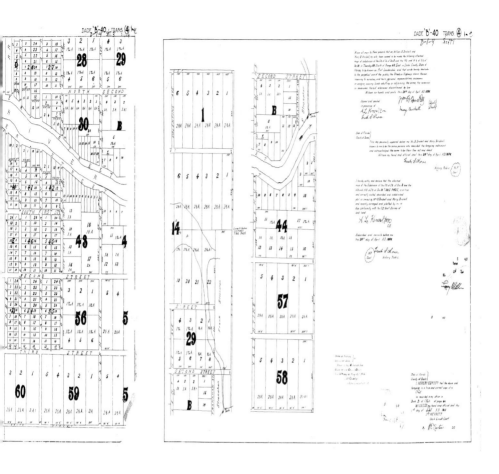

future, the town of Fort Lauderdale plat was recorded with the Dade County Circuit Court.

With the arrival of speedy and reliable rail transportation to northern markets, the Fort Lauderdale area became a major supplier of produce, mostly citrus and tomatoes, some of which was barged down New River from the rich-soil farmlands to the west. Those who migrated to the area to work the farms, processing plants, and other emerging businesses brought with them their families, and by 1899, there were enough children in the town to justify a school. Town leaders petitioned the Dade County School Board, which ruled that if the citizens built a schoolhouse, it would send a teacher. Townsfolk constructed a one-room schoolhouse at the corner of today's South Andrews Avenue and 5th Street, and Miss Ivy Julia Cromartie from Lemon City was hired as its first teacher.[127]

Opposite, top left: The one-room schoolhouse built by the townsfolk on South Andrews Avenue at today's Southwest 5th Street. *Courtesy of History Fort Lauderdale.*

Opposite, top right: Miss Ivy Julie Cromartie with her students, circa 1899. *Courtesy of the Maitland Collection, Broward County Historical Archives, Broward County Libraries.*

Opposite, bottom: The Bryan House was featured in an advertisement in Model Land Company's July 1, 1899 magazine. The advertisement read, "For sale on New River with railroad passing through centre. Trains daily. Has 1 hotel (Bryan House, pictured), etc. Rich fruit and trucking lands. Promises to settle up quickly. Lots $50 to $250." *Photograph courtesy of History Fort Lauderdale.*

Above: Miss Cromartie, who was courted by and married Frank Stranahan. *Boating photograph by Frank Stranahan, courtesy of History Fort Lauderdale, portrait courtesy of the State Archives of Florida.*

The "comely and vivacious" Miss Cromartie quickly attracted the attention of Frank Stranahan, a young man who was stranded in an area with no eligible young ladies. "Certainly, the camp manager and Indian trader was considered the 'best prospect' among the eligible bachelors," wrote Harry Kersey. And after a quick courtship, the two were married in 1900.[128] Their impact on Fort Lauderdale is legendary.

"The days of leisurely settlement on New River were coming to an end," Kersey wrote. Few could imagine how quickly life would change.

9

BECOMING THE
"VENICE OF AMERICA"

Fifty years before Frank and Ivy Stranahan said their vows at the bride's family home in Lemon City, the federal government triggered a series of events that would ultimately transform the state of Florida from a tropical escape from cold winters to a home for approximately 22 million people at the time of this writing. (There are almost 2 million people living in Broward County alone.)

The twice-daily dance between the natural southeasterly flow of the Everglades and the tidal rise and fall of the Atlantic Ocean maintained a healthy balance that kept the river of grass from overflowing the coastal ridge that runs down the center of today's Fort Lauderdale. That ridge, though, was just a few miles wide. Everything west of today's I-95 was Everglades swampland; everything east of Colee Hammock was a nearly impenetrable mangrove swamp, wet with the tides, impeding access to New River Sound, the barrier island, and the Atlantic Ocean.

The fate of the Everglades was set the same year Florida became a state: 1845. One of the new legislature's first acts was to petition Congress to study the Everglades for the purpose of reclamation. Two years later, civil engineer Buckingham Smith of St. Augustine was appointed to determine if reclamation could be achieved by draining the Everglades. As reported by Marjory Stoneman Douglas: "The water of the Everglades would easily run off, [Smith] wrote, once the rock that held it in place was cut through. Beyond some little stench of decaying vegetation, it would be attended with no ill effects and should cost about $500,000."[129] Congress soon passed the

Swamp and Overflowed Land Grant Act of 1850, which enabled Florida and other states "to reclaim the swamplands" within their borders.

In Florida, about twenty million acres were eventually granted to the state from the federal government; of this, about 25 percent was considered part of the Everglades. In a bit of circular logic that would plague Florida's real estate reputation for generations to come, the act authorized the state to sell the swamplands before they were drained in order to raise money to drain them. Swampland sales were also used to finance other "internal improvements" to help populate the southernmost state. To administer this vast undertaking and collect the millions of dollars it would raise, in 1855, the Florida legislature created the Trustees of the Internal Improvement Fund.

A renewed focus on the swamplands, the Everglades in particular, led Florida citizens, land speculators, and political leaders, all with dollar signs in their eyes, to revisit the issue of the unconquered Natives, who numbered some three hundred to four hundred by that time. Most were living peacefully in their villages deep in the river of grass. Left alone since the end of the Second Seminole War (1842), they were again cast as an impediment to progress.

Attempting once again to force the Natives to leave their relatively comfortable, safe, and productive lands in Florida for reservations in the Midwest, U.S. secretary of war Jefferson Davis tried a different approach—starve them out. He instituted embargoes against Native trade, cutting off needed supplies and the money to pay for them. Billy Bowlegs, the chief of most of the remaining Seminole bands and a leader who was experienced in the terrors of war, tried to maintain the fragile peace, rounding up a few renegade Natives who had killed and pillaged outside the reservation and turning them over to the White authorities. Unimpressed with the chief's efforts, the government increased the pressure, sending soldiers and surveyors into Seminole reservations to map out future White farms and homesteads. One account, which is unproven, said that an army survey crew deliberately destroyed Bowlegs's banana grove. Whether that story is true or not, Billy Bowlegs and the other chiefs were fed up and led thirty warriors to attack a nearby army unit at 5:00 a.m. on December 18, 1855. The Third Seminole War had begun.[130]

It ended three years later in the same manner as the previous two—a stalemate. While Billy Bowlegs and some of his followers agreed to leave Florida for the Native reservations, unknown hundreds remained peacefully in their Everglades home.

But soon, the nation and the citizens of Florida were consumed with another matter, one that would tear apart the fragile fabric of the young republic. On January 11, 1861, Florida seceded from the Union and, the following month, joined six other Southern states to create the Confederate States of America. Four months later, the Civil War began. "The hazy plans for reclaiming the Everglades by draining them were locked in the state archives," wrote Douglas.[131]

The plans remained in dusty drawers until 1880, when the federal government again nudged Florida with a grant of over two million acres of swamplands within the state's borders to encourage the construction of internal improvements.[132] Those two million acres were added to the lands that were already in the state's coffers, all of which were tied up in post–Civil War litigation, leaving the Internal Improvement Fund land rich and cash poor. To break the stalemate, Hamilton Disston, the son of a wealthy Philadelphia saw manufacturer with grand ambitions of becoming a Florida land baron, purchased four million acres of swampland from the state at a reported cost of $0.25 per acre. With that $1 million, the state resolved its financial quagmire, freeing up its remaining millions of acres of swampland to be used as payment for other internal improvements, such as railroads, drainage canals, and waterways.

On March 8, 1881, the state granted a charter to a company controlled by Disston to "drain a large expanse of the Everglades and develop an Atlantic Intracoastal Waterway," wrote William Crawford.[133] Instead of focusing his drainage efforts on the Everglades south of Lake Okeechobee, Disston instead concentrated on the areas to its north and west. Perhaps he reasoned that if he could divert a substantial volume of water before it got to the southern rim of the lake, the Everglades would dry. He dredged a canal, connecting the western shore of the lake to the Gulf of Mexico via the Caloosahatchee River. While Disston's work reclaimed millions of acres of swampland on the northwest side of the lake (and earned about two million acres for himself), it had little to no effect on the Everglades proper. The water still flowed south, and the Everglades remained wet. Development in southeast Florida continued to be squeezed on the narrow coastal ridge.

As for the assignment of Disston to develop an Atlantic Intracoastal Waterway, that challenge had already been reassigned in 1881 to the aforementioned Florida Coast Line Canal and Transportation Company.

"As Florida entered the twentieth century, the Everglades was as primeval as it had been when Buckingham Smith surveyed it in 1848," wrote Cooper Kirk. In 1900, the few poor inland settlers "found themselves at the mercy of the water, which flowed eastward from the Everglades and inundated their crops and primitive dwellings. Flooded fields and dwellings left them bewildered."[134] It took a new governor with an unusual name and atypical pedigree to supercharge the drainage dreams.

Napoleon Bonaparte Broward Jr. was born in 1857, the second of nine children, at his family's modest plantation on Cedar Creek (south of today's Jacksonville International Airport). Educated and well read, "the Browards liked historic and fancy names," explained Broward's biographer, Samuel Proctor, a distinguished service professor emeritus of history at the University of Florida. Napoleon's younger brother was named Montcalm, apparently for the French general who was the North American commander of the Seven Years' War (1756–1763).

When one hears the name Napoleon Bonaparte, they may conjure up the image of the French commander: short, stout, prissy, pale, and overdressed in ruffled shirts, velvet jackets, and fancy hats. However, Florida's Napoleon Bonaparte Broward was anything but. As a teenager, "his body was hard and swift"; by his late twenties, he was a large, imposing man, "his two hundred ten pounds well distributed over his six-foot-two-inch frame," described Proctor. "A mustache, thick and neatly trimmed in the fashion of the day, adorned his full face. Long hours in the hot sun had browned his complexion and had given a smoldering redness to his dark hair." He had a no-nonsense demeanor and walked with an alert, almost military step.[135]

The Browards were relatively prosperous farmers prior to the Civil

Napoleon Bonaparte Broward. *Courtesy of the Jacksonville Historical Society.*

War, but when the Federal army invaded the northern part of the state in 1862, the Browards escaped their Jacksonville-area plantation and moved to a small cabin they owned in White Springs, about sixty-five miles to the west. When they returned after the war, they were desperately poor. "Their slaves had been freed; their home, crops, and cattle, and most of their personal possessions had been burned, destroyed, or stolen. Unable to pay the heavy taxes levied by the 'carpetbag' administration in Florida, they saw huge tracts of their land sacrificed on the auction block in Jacksonville."[136]

Starting over, the Browards built a small log house using tools they had carried from their White Springs refuge, and they tried farming their remaining land on Cedar Creek, producing not nearly enough food for a family of eleven. Mrs. Broward died in 1869; her daughters were sent to live with their aunts, leaving the young boys behind with their father to tend the deteriorating farm. It was a lonely life. After supper, the boys would park their guns and bowie knives within quick reach of their beds before they went to sleep. Their father died when Napoleon was fourteen, and the boys moved to their uncle's lumber camp at Mill Cove, just off the St. Johns River east of Jacksonville. "Napoleon's job was to raft logs after they had been cut by the loggers and brought to the river with horse teams," Proctor explained. There, his love of the river was born. He left school in 1875 to work on a St. Johns River steamboat, where, after failing as a cook, "he was made assistant fireman and then worked as a deckhand and wheelman." After a three-year stint on big boats up north, he returned to Florida, continuing his progression as a mate and then riverboat captain. In 1883, he married, got his commission as a St. Johns River Bar pilot (a prestigious and lucrative profession), and partnered with another captain to build a steamer. "The winter was a banner one for the river boats," said Proctor.

> *The St. Johns, like other rivers of northeast Florida during the 1880s, swarmed with steamboats of every description, ranging from small, odd-looking craft that ran to places far up the river, to the fastest and most-modern passenger boats. With orange trees in full bearing in the groves and plantations along the waterway, and with few railroads south of Jacksonville to offer freight competition, river-boat captains like Broward found the shipping of oranges a lucrative business.*[137]

(The St. Johns is one of the few rivers in the country that flows from south to north. An excursion "far up the river" would be to the south.)

At age thirty-one, Broward's life took an unexpected turn, setting a new course for his future. "A notorious forger from New York, who had absconded with forty thousand dollars, was arrested in Jacksonville and lodged in the city jail," Proctor explained. For some reason, the Duval County sheriff transferred the crook to a luxury suite of rooms in a nearby hotel, where he was guarded by two deputies (this decision was subject to abundant after-the-fact speculation). During the long, quiet night, the deputies dozed, and the forger flew. Furious, the governor fired the sheriff and sought recommendations for his replacement, seeking a man who was "thoroughly sober and of good moral character." Having led just such a life, Napoleon

Bonaparte Broward was appointed the Duval County sheriff in February 1888. Within weeks, his moral fortitude was proven in a crusade against illegal gambling in Jacksonville. Arresting the perpetrators and fending off attempts to bribe him (including a large roll of bills left in his office, which Broward turned over to prosecutors), the bad guys were convicted, and Broward's political reputation was cemented. "By the end of 1891, Broward had become one of the popular and prominent men in Florida." State newspapers carried stories of his daring arrests and civic character, while at the same time, he "was developing a broad interest in civic affairs and in the social and business life of his community."[138]

While Broward was building his bona fides, sea change was taking place in the Florida capital. Since the end of Reconstruction in 1877, statewide politics had been dominated by a relatively few big corporate and railroad interests, including, Proctor said, "men like Henry Bradley Plant, Hamilton Disston, Henry Morrison Flagler." The corporations led by these men and others held millions of acres of state land, which was either granted or sold at a discount by the legislature for improvements designed to stimulate population and economic growth. But many of the state's farmers, laborers, and shopkeepers felt that the government was lining the pockets of big northern businessmen at their expense. It was a festering wound.

By the end of the nineteenth century, the state was split, battle lines drawn. On one side were the corporations, easily personified by the railroads crisscrossing the state. On the other side was the working and farming class. True to his upbringing, Broward cast his lot with the working folks. In an open letter to the press on July 20, 1894, he claimed four railroads "had established an interstate transportation monopoly, which was costing Florida approximately four hundred thousand dollars a year." Broward's position was that the railroads manipulated local rates on oranges and phosphate shipments, driving up costs for working Floridians, while increasing railroad profits.[139]

In 1895, Broward parlayed his populist views into higher office with his election to the Duval County council, winning with an overwhelming majority of votes thanks in part to the unqualified endorsement of the *Florida Times-Union*. Support from the de facto state newspaper greased Broward's influence throughout Florida. He rode his popularity to the state legislature in 1900, and then, in 1903, he set his sights on the governor's mansion, broadening his anti-corporate and anti-railroad platform to include the mantra of draining the Everglades for its panacea of rich farmland. "Never bashful, and often daring, Broward trumpeted the claim that the Everglades contained the richest soil in the world and that its conquest could supply, among other things, all the sugar cane needed by the United States," said Cooper Kirk. With the reclaimed Everglades serving the nation's pantry, "all Floridians would profit, and some would grow rich."[140] In downhome language and armed on the campaign trail with a portfolio of visuals—graphs, pictures, and a large map of south Florida—Broward detailed the basics of the reclamation program. When challenged about the feasibility of drainage, he brandished the large map, pointed to the center of the Everglades, stated that it was twenty-one feet above sea level, and, with schoolboy logic, cited the seemingly obvious—"Water will run downhill!"[141]

The Democratic primary battle was hard fought. Broward's opponent (Robert W. Davis), who was favored in the cities, was considered too strong to be defeated by a "former farm boy and deckhand with no schooling."[142] But Broward's barnstorming in rural areas and his natural appeal to the countryfolk won the day. In the general election, neither candidate from the Republican nor the Socialist Party constituted a serious threat to the powerful Democrats. Broward won in a landslide and was inaugurated on January 3, 1905.

A half century of drainage dreamers had found a new and powerful champion. Broward quickly convinced a reluctant legislature to pass sweeping laws, authorizing and governing the drainage and reclamation of the Everglades. The first canals to be dredged were from New River, where the Everglades was closest to the Atlantic. To say that the governor was firmly in charge was an understatement. "From his home city of Jacksonville, he had materials shipped to New River," wrote Kirk. "He journeyed to Chicago and purchased engines for dredges," then traveled to Fort Lauderdale, where he stayed at Philemon Bryan's New River Inn and monitored the construction of two powerful dredges just across the river.[143]

Broward and his family were in Fort Lauderdale in July 1906 to christen the first dredge, the *Everglades*. It was a festive affair—the obligatory bottle of champagne was smashed across the boat's bow. With a beam of forty-two feet, the eighty-foot-long boat was powered by a five-hundred-horsepower engine and was quickly put to work heading northwest from New River's north fork, with Captain Reed Asa Bryan Sr. at the helm.[144] The launch of the *Okeechobee* followed in similar fashion a month later, and by summer 1907, the two powerful dredges were at work cutting canals through the swamp from New River's north and south forks. With no detailed survey to follow, engineering parties often had to hack their way through "saw grass six to eight feet tall and so thick a snake would have had to bend his

Philemon Bryan's New River Inn, circa 1917. *Courtesy of the State Archives of Florida.*

crooked back to get through….Surveyors used a long, narrow boat to carry supplies, eats, and bedding. These were drawn by men who would cut by hand and clear the right of way of grass, brush, and any trees so surveyors could set stakes and run lines," wrote the chief engineer for the drainage project, Fred Cotton Elliot.[145] The surveyors were followed close behind by the massive dredges.

But in the midst of all the excitement, reality suddenly struck. The Internal Improvement Fund, the state agency that paid for the dredging, went broke. Special drainage taxes on private landholdings, authorized by the legislature, were tied up in litigation. The fund's portfolio was rich with over two and a half million acres of land but no cash. "Sell the Everglades," was Broward's order.

And so, south Florida's new future began, personified by a flamboyant land huckster named Richard J. "Dicky" Bolles, who purchased five hundred thousand acres of Florida swampland for $1 million. Described as the most-spectacular, most-ingenious, and most-criticized promotor of Everglades land, Bolles's swampland sales scheme was described in detail in the Fort Lauderdale history *Checkered Sunshine*:

> *Richard Bolles divided his Everglades holdings into twelve thousand tracts of ten to six hundred and forty acres* [a section] *and set up a unique selling plan. He advertised nationally, and as an added inducement included a lot in Progresso,* [a subdivision on dry land] *in Fort Lauderdale….* *Contracts for a minimum ten-acre tract, with a Progresso lot included, were offered for two hundred and forty dollars each at the rate of ten dollars per*

Florida's chief engineer for the Everglades drainage project, Fred C. Elliot (*right*), often joined survey crews in six-to-eight-foot-tall sawgrass. Perhaps the photographer wanted a tamer location for this image. *Courtesy of the State Archives of Florida.*

Above: Walker S. Holloway (*foreground, left*), captain of the *Okeechobee*, with guests as they cruise on a newly dredged Everglades canal. *Courtesy of History Fort Lauderdale.*

Right: The dredge *Okeechobee* at work. *Courtesy of the W.S. Holloway Collection, Broward County Historical Archives, Broward County Libraries.*

month. Thousands of contracts were sold. The purchasers were also to have the opportunity, at a huge drawing to be held in Fort Lauderdale in March of 1911, of acquiring as much as a section instead of the minimum ten acres guaranteed by their purchases.[146]

Before the land lottery, the small settlement of Fort Lauderdale had had about 150 residents. They were swamped by an estimated 3,000 people, most from the Midwest, packed in a tent city with lottery-fueled dreams of becoming land barons in the new frontier.

With all of the out-of-towners, local business was booming. The New River Inn was sold out, and lines were long at the few local eateries. Stranahan's trading post, which was moved upriver a short distance when he built his new residence in 1901, had difficulty keeping shelves stocked. "Prosperity, hithertofore undreamed, lay just around the corner," wrote Weidling and Burghard. Bolles and his land hucksters were local heroes. With cash boxes flush, basic services strained, and primitive infrastructure overwhelmed by the flood of people—but with optimism—settlement leaders incorporated the Town of Fort Lauderdale on March 27, 1911.

While town leaders were celebrating Dicky Bolles, law enforcement up north was suspicious. Reacting to complaints across northern cities,

Frenzied visitors packed a hastily erected tent city for the great land lottery in 1911. *Courtesy of History Fort Lauderdale.*

115

particularly in the Midwest where sales had been the greatest, that citizens had been hustled into buying swampland, the federal government investigated and indicted Bolles on 112 counts of "using the mails to advertise a lottery" and of false advertising for his claim that the swampland would become habitable. Undeterred and unshakable, Bolles remained in Florida and the cases dragged on. He died in 1917 of natural causes on an FEC train that he had boarded at Palm Beach—destination unknown. His case never went to court.[147]

Limited to only one four-year term, Broward left public office in 1909. Many thought the crusading campaigner and governor would have personally profited from his public endeavors, as many did during his time and today. Yet, when he left office, he was poorer than when he became governor. That didn't stop him from running for the United States Senate, winning the 1910 election. But exhausted from years of Tallahassee politics, his relentless statewide barnstorming in support of his drainage project, and his Senate campaign, Broward "was an easy prey to disease." He died on October 1, 1910, before he was sworn into his Senate seat, at the age of fifty-three. His biographer, Samuel Proctor, eulogized him as one of Florida's most courageous governors.[148]

With Broward gone, the work to drain and populate the Everglades continued, albeit without the same passion and prose. Remaining in the coffers of the Internal Improvement Fund were millions of dollars that had been paid by Bolles and other land speculators, most earmarked for Everglades drainage. Even though canal digging began at both the north and south forks of New River, it was the south fork that eventually reached Lake Okeechobee. Confusingly named North New River Canal, current-day highways I-595 and U.S. 27 follow its route.

On April 26, 1912, "every man, woman, and child" in the Town of Fort Lauderdale turned out when Broward's successor, Governor Albert W. Gilchrist, and Mayor William H. Marshall officially opened the North New River Canal to Okeechobee.[149] The canal, like those that would soon follow, was, at the time, as much a transportation artery as a drainage canal, explained Kirk. "Shallow draft canal boats transported passengers, household goods, fertilizer, and seeds to the lake region and returned with vegetables, fish, and livestock." Already booming with cash and new settlers from Dicky Bolles's land lottery, the frontier town of Fort Lauderdale became the epicenter of Lake Okeechobee canal traffic. New settlements, like Zona (soon renamed Davie), popped up along its previously inaccessible banks. Real estate companies developed new schemes to sell their abundant—if still

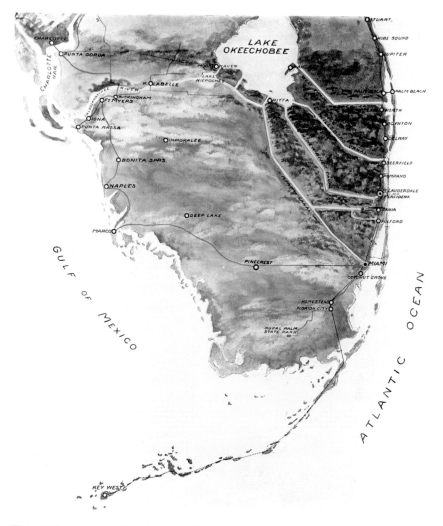

This 1924 map of the Okeechobee drainage canals shows the North New River Canal in reference to the other major canals. *Courtesy of the State Archives of Florida.*

wet—lots. One offered free homes to purchasers of twenty acres of land; the small homes were fabricated in Miami and carted to Davie to be erected by the new owners.

Tempering the enthusiasm were persistent and growing rumors that the Everglades was not cooperating. Homesites and fields were awash with the summer rains. Even downstream, the new bungalow dwellers in Davie often arose to find water at their doorsteps. This was no longer Bolles's problem—the state and its governor had emphatically said draining the

Governor Albert W. Gilchrist (*in black suit*) with Fort Lauderdale mayor William M. Marshall at the ceremonial opening of the North New River Canal at the foot of Brickell Avenue. The handwritten caption on the photo celebrates it as a "gateway connecting Gulf to Atlantic." *Courtesy of the State Archives of Florida.*

Everglades would be easy. In an attempt to mitigate legal and public relations problems, new canals were dredged, increasing the outbound water flow, but as it had for thousands of years, the Everglades remained a swamp.

Kicking that can down the soggy road, the city fathers in Fort Lauderdale began thinking about making the town more than just a waypoint for growing and shipping agricultural products. They looked with envy at the thriving tourism business in Palm Beach and the evolving one in Miami. But both of those destinations had amenities Fort Lauderdale was missing—easy access to the beach and facilities for enjoying the excursion. To get to the beach in Fort Lauderdale, one had to take a precarious trek through a mangrove swamp and a daredevil swim or boat ride across New River Sound (which was famous for sharks), before reaching the white sand beach on the desolate barrier island. In 1914, local businesses took the lead in building facilities on the

Dredge in the distance making headway toward Lake Okeechobee. *Courtesy Napoleon Broward Collection, Broward County Historical Archives, Broward County Libraries.*

beach, including a two-story pavilion with restrooms, changing rooms and showers, a refreshment stand, and a dance floor. But there was one small problem: there was no road or bridge to get there.

Mary Brickell came to the rescue, improving the value of her land at the same time. She built an east–west road (today's Las Olas Boulevard) through her property to a wooden bridge that was constructed by the city over the sound. It opened to great fanfare in January 1917. The bridge had a pivoting section in the middle to allow boat traffic; it was rotated by the bridge tender, who turned a large key in a slot in the middle of the span. This was a cumbersome and time-consuming process to be sure, but it was done with no complaint. At last, Fort Lauderdale had a beach.

In 1913, local resident D.C. Alexander stopped his automobile on East Las Olas Boulevard near Colee Hammock to take this photograph. Soon, construction crews built a modern road and bridge to the beach along this route. *Courtesy of History Fort Lauderdale.*

Flush with population and financial growth, Fort Lauderdale, Davie, Deerfield, Dania, Hallandale, and the emerging town of Pompano split off from Palm Beach and Dade Counties to form their own county, named after the governor who had meant so much to their future. Broward County became a reality on October 1, 1915, with an official population of 4,763 people over 1,230 square miles—some 80 percent still covered by the watery Everglades.[150] A portion of that 80 percent had been purchased to be farmed when the state-promised drainage became reality; other soggy portions were owned by speculators who were content to hold their unimproved property until the land was dry and the demand would increase its value.

1920

Finally, Fort Lauderdale had an accessible beach. *Courtesy of History Fort Lauderdale.*

A glimpse of spring breaks to come? Bathers at Las Olas Beach. *Courtesy of the State of Florida Archives.*

From a municipal budget prospective, unimproved land was a liability. Without improvements, property taxes were minuscule. That left a dilemma for officials of the newly created Broward County. Needing to increase its tax base to fund the road and bridge construction that was necessary for growth, but with habitable land confined to the narrow coastal ridge, leaders looked for ways to create more valuable and immediately buildable homesites. What is true today was true then—access to waterways increases property values and tax revenues. Accepting that fact, city leaders, both elected and de facto, met in the office of *Fort Lauderdale Sentinel* publisher George G. Matthews to brainstorm how waterways could be the key to growth and prosperity for Broward County. The meeting was memorialized in an editorial on September 12, 1916:

> *There is no place on the east coast of Florida that presents the possibilities for a paradise on earth that is offered by the land along New River.*
>
> *A visionary group, dreamers if you are pleased to call the group, were gathered in the* Sentinel *office last Tuesday, discussing the tidelands laying between Fort Lauderdale and the* [New River Sound]. *The idea of these "dreamers" is that by dredging out canals and cross canals 30 to 100 feet wide through these flats, the silt and debris from the canals being used to raise the level of the rest of the land several feet, they will have built numerous small islands surrounded by the fresh running waters of New River.*
>
> *These little islands of every conceivable shape and size would not be merely on the bay front but would be literally surrounded by waters of the bay and river with the tides of the Atlantic rising and falling in the streets of this modern Venice, the winter resort of the wealthy of the nation.*[151]

Thus, Fort Lauderdale became the "Venice of America," with 165 miles of navigable waterways, most man-made, within its limits. The commensurate rise in real estate values prompted Mary Brickell to capitalize on her huge property investments. On March 22, 1920, she platted a subdivision composed of nearly half of the old Frankee Lewis Donation. She named it Colee Hammock.

Why did Mary Brickell name her new subdivision Colee Hammock? The author of this book asked Fort Lauderdale lawyer, historian, and author William Crawford this question. He said that when civil engineers of the period needed names for roads and landmarks, they often used the names of early residents, landowners, prominent citizens, and acquaintances

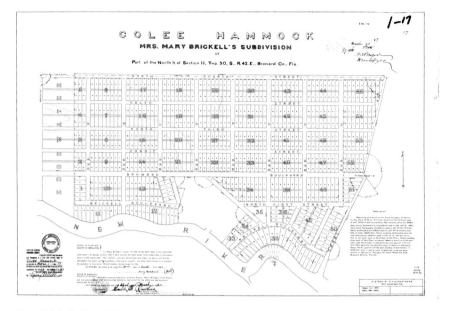

Mary Brickell platted Colee Hammock on March 22, 1920. Her steadfast protection of the property from highways and railways resulted in it becoming one of the city's most desired historic neighborhoods. *Provided by Broward County Engineering Department.*

of those creating the plats. For example, on the original 1896 town of Fort Lauderdale plat, the name "Colee Avenue" was placed on today's Northwest and Southwest 7th Avenue. In a written note found in the Fort Lauderdale Historical Society archives, early Fort Lauderdale settler Mrs. H.G. Wheeler said that Colee Avenue was "named for James A. [*sic*] Colee of St. Augustine, a surveyor and woodsman for the East Coast Canal Co. at the time of cutting canal from Lake Worth to New River, 1893 to 1895."[152] Historian Dr. Cooper Kirk confirmed that a canal workcamp at Tarpon Bend, the heart of Colee Hammock, was named for James Louis Colee, the canal company's engineer.[153] In 1891, Colee became a New River–area landowner, purchasing 594 acres along the Florida Coast Line Canal, including 40 acres near today's Port Everglades.[154] Whether Mary Brickell knew Colee is unknown, but all of these facts lead to the conclusion that when civil engineer H.C. Davis created the Colee Hammock plat in 1920, he carried forth the name of James Louis Colee.

As the 1920s roared in, Fort Lauderdale's success seemed unlimited. It fulfilled its claim as the Gateway to the Everglades, ferrying thousands of crates carrying fruits and vegetables from the farms around Lake Okeechobee

Andrews Avenue, "main street" Fort Lauderdale, circa 1926. *Courtesy of the State Archives of Florida.*

downriver to the railway wharves in town, where it was then shipped to eager markets up north. The only known factor inhibiting growth of the agriculture industry was the increasing expense of railway shipping. Water transportation on the Florida Coast Line Canal was an option, but it was slow and subject to weather, shoaling, and other impediments. The Florida East Coast Railway provided the only speedy and reliable shipping option for outbound produce from the farms and inbound construction materials that were needed by the fast-growing town. As the only game in town, the railway controlled its rates, and its revenue skyrocketed.

With little leverage against the railway, Broward County officials started thinking about adding embellishments to the Florida Coast Line Canal (today's Atlantic Intracoastal Waterway), settling on the creation of a deep-water public seaport that catered to both yachtsmen and commercial interests. Officials had found the perfect place for it on the canal's west side south of New River Inlet. It was called Lake Mabel and was originally a shallow brackish lake covering nearly four thousand acres that was formed when ocean water spilled across the skinny barrier island. There's a story about how the lake got its name that is told in a document written by Arthur T. Williams, the son of pioneer south Florida surveyor Marcellus A. Williams. The article recalled Arthur's travels with his father on late 1800s surveying trips, alerting the young man to some attractive real estate opportunities. In 1893, Arthur and a friend, James A. Harris, purchased a large parcel of land south of New River Sound, which included a large lake. When Harris asked Arthur the name of the lake, he said it didn't have one, "but that [he] was going to name it for his sweetheart, Miss Mabel White, whom he soon after married." Later, Arthur and Major J.W. Bushnell collaborated on a new map of Florida, "and on that map, [they] named the lake 'Mabel,'" which is how it remained until it became the centerpiece of a massive new enterprise.[155]

While Fort Lauderdale's leaders were contemplating the new seaport, by 1926, Joseph W. Young, a land developer and founder of the adjacent town

Lake Mabel, circa 1925, destined for a new life as the "Gateway to the World." *Courtesy of History Fort Lauderdale.*

Above: Preparing to dynamite the final sandbar between Lake Mabel and the Atlantic Ocean. *Courtesy of the State Archives of Florida.*

Left: Celebrating Port Everglades at Bay Mabel. (Lake Mabel was often referred to as Bay Mabel.) *Courtesy of History Fort Lauderdale.*

of Hollywood, was one step ahead, announcing his own plans for a deep-water harbor in Lake Mabel. The plan, he reasoned, would open the door not just to northern U.S. markets, but to other countries as well. Rather than argue about which town's plan should proceed, Hollywood and Fort Lauderdale joined forces to create the port, and on February 22, 1928, "an elaborate celebration marked the dynamiting of the final sand bar between then–Lake Mabel and the Atlantic Ocean." With schools and businesses closed, an estimated 85 percent of Broward County residents attended the dramatic opening, which was billed as a "Wedding of the Waters."[156]

Success came quickly—in the first year of operation, $100,000 worth of products (about $1,520,000 in today's dollars) were shipped from the port to Cuba, the Caribbean, and Latin America.[157] Port Everglades at Lake Mabel was on its way, as was the bright future of the town that grew up on the shores of New River.

TODAY'S NEW RIVER

S trolling down Riverwalk on the north side of today's New River, it is hard to imagine how it looked when the family of Bahamians Surles and Frankee Lewis settled on its banks sometime before 1793. Thankfully, due to the good work of local historians, writers, the Fort Lauderdale Historical Society, and the Broward County Historical Archives, we have detailed descriptions of a crystal clear river that varied in depth from three to twenty feet in a tropical jungle where wild animals roamed free.[158] And thanks to generations of researchers and storytellers, dating back to the original settlers, we have a vision of life along New River—its triumphs and tragedies. Through Dr. Cooper Kirk's heart-wrenching narrative, we can taste the horror of the 1836 Cooley family murders near the river's north and south forks.

Consider the decades before bridges crossed the water, when the enterprising Frank Stranahan was sent to New River to build and manage an overnight tent camp and ferry service for the passengers of his cousin's new stagecoach line from Lake Worth to the settlement that was then known as Lemon City on Biscayne Bay. For most of us, it is even harder to go back centuries and imagine the Natives, presumed to be Tequestas camped in the area, who may have witnessed the "thundering noises and the ground trembling beneath them," creating the "mighty and majestic river" they called "Himmarshee," which is believed to mean "New Water."[159] It's hard to imagine later years when the young boys of the emerging town tossed two-by-fours into a whirlpool at Sailboat Bend, amazed when they resurfaced a mile downriver at Tarpon Bend. The river's mysterious whirlpools are now silted up by runoff from the North New River Canal to the Everglades, part of an enormous dredging project to "drain the Everglades" and "reclaim" millions of acres of newly habitable land while creating an environmental challenge for all of central and south Florida that, at the time of this writing, is still far from resolution.

A year before Flagler's railroad made its inaugural run from West Palm Beach to the small settlement on New River, the area was opened to ports north via the Florida Coast Line Canal (today's Atlantic Intracoastal Waterway), offering safe inland passage for passengers and products aboard vessels both small and large.

The railroad was the pivot point between the past and the present on Florida's southeast coast. Its first passengers arrived at Fort Lauderdale Station (named for the military fort) in February 1896. Two months later, the town of Fort Lauderdale plat maps were drawn; fifteen years later, its charter was approved by the Florida Legislature. In 1915, Broward County was carved out of Dade and Palm Beach Counties, named for former Florida governor Napoleon Bonaparte Broward, who championed draining the Everglades.

Today, a cruise up New River via private boat, chartered yacht, water taxi, Italian gondola, or sightseeing riverboat reveals a river that is no longer a wilderness paradise, but the hardworking heart of a thriving, vibrant city. The river's current still runs at a brisk three to four knots, with a twice-daily tidal change of two to three feet. Multimillion-dollar yachts are wedged bow to stern outside multimillion-dollar mansions; yet, much of the river is still accessible to the public along Riverwalk, a brick-lined one-and-a-half-mile-long, eighteen-acre promenade with parks, plazas, and gazebos. Dock-and-dine restaurants are intermingled with chichi stores and spas, and paddleboard and kayak concessions serve the adventurous. Captains of smaller boats will find a public ramp at Cooley's Landing, near the original homestead and coontie processing plant of William Cooley, the actual site of the Cooley family killings.

Those whose view of the river is confined to downtown's stores, restaurants, and high-rises, as well as pleasure boaters whose cruises may end before the river splits into north and south forks, are missing a vital element of New River's contributions to Broward County. About two and a half nautical miles upriver, near where the river passes under I-95, the banks transform from mid-century waterfront homes to acres of immaculate boatyards

While cruising southwest on New River's south fork or glancing down from the mammoth I-95 flyover, one discovers Lauderdale Marine Center. It is said to be the largest yacht repair facility and shipyard in the United States and is part of Broward County's $9 billion marine industry. *Courtesy of Christopher Savage, Savage Global Marketing.*

where multimillion-dollar superyachts come from all over the world for maintenance, refitting, and to be made even grander. It is estimated that this hidden gem, associated marine industries, and sales of boats both big and small contribute $9 billion a year to Broward County's economy and employ over 112,000 people, most in small local businesses and many who were trained in local public and private trade schools. The annual Fort Lauderdale Boat Show, which will celebrate its sixty-first season at the time of this book's publication, attracts over 100,000 guests from around the world each year.[160]

Today, in 2020, Broward County's population is around two million, and the vast majority of its residents are from somewhere else. New River's legends and lore are mostly unknown or have long been forgotten; its "massacre" is only commemorated by a stone-and-brass monument that is still standing at the wrong place. Its military forts are gone, lost with the bones of the Cooley family, Natives, settlers, slaves, and soldiers, beneath neighborhoods and high-rise buildings. New arrivals and visitors aboard the "world-famous" *Jungle Queen* and other sightseeing cruises on New River will have a good time, but they won't learn much history, as the cruises are focused on the homes of the rich and relatively famous. But *real history* can still be found along New River. Tucked on its north bank, where U.S. 1 dips beneath the river, is the modest Stranahan House,

The past comes to life at History Fort Lauderdale on Southwest 2nd Avenue at the riverfront. *Author's collection.*

which is now restored and preserved as a museum. Nearby, the FEC Railway still punctuates its presence, crossing the river on an enormous drawbridge. Across Southwest 2nd Avenue from the tracks, the past comes alive at History Fort Lauderdale, which includes the 1905 New River Inn (the settlement's first hotel and now a museum of local history), as well as other historic homes and the Fort Lauderdale Historical Society's public research library and archives.

Colee Hammock, which comprises much of the old Frankee Lewis Donation, is now described as a "historic and highly desirable waterfront neighborhood of multi-million-dollar single-family homes that exude old Florida charm." Along the waterfront at Tarpon Bend is the historic Colee Hammock Park, a peaceful place for quiet riverfront reflection.

Today's Port Everglades exceeds even the wildest dreams of its founders. The third-largest cruise port in the world in 2019, with ten cruise lines serving almost four million passengers a year, Port Everglades is also a major supplier of the state's energy needs, with more than 120 million barrels of petroleum products arriving in 2019. Located a half mile from Atlantic shipping lanes, it is the tenth-busiest container port in the nation.[161] With

Colee Hammock Park at Tarpon Bend, a peaceful public refuge on the river. The Cooley Massacre monument is under the old oak tree. *Author's collection.*

A luxury cruise ship enters the Port Everglades canal near the location where the final sandbar was broken through to open the port in 1928. *Courtesy of Port Everglades.*

The mile-long Riverwalk is billed as "Florida's Most Beautiful Mile." *Author's collection.*

Port Everglades, Fort Lauderdale became not only the Gateway to the Everglades, but a gateway to the world.

For those who would like to experience a little of what New River was like before it was tamed, they can visit the Bill Keith Preserve, a three-acre wilderness on the south fork of the river. While it has been made accessible with walking trails and a few picnic tables, the thick vegetation and mangrove-lined shores are much like those that were encountered by the first Native explorers.

With success comes struggle. Like most heavily populated regions in Florida, New River and its surrounding areas face environmental and infrastructural challenges that were unimagined by their founders and, in many cases, ignored by the leaders who followed. As an example of the pressures of growth and time, shortly before the last pages of this book were written in early 2020, water and sewer pipes under downtown Fort Lauderdale's high-rises and homes burst, compromised by age, seawater encroachment, and overuse, spewing over two hundred million gallons of raw wastewater into streets, canals, and New River itself. City officials were considering taking the drastic step of enforcing a construction moratorium to give them time to repair and replace the pipes under the overdeveloped downtown, and in June 2020, the State of Florida issued $2.1 million in fines for the spills, the largest in state history.[162]

Yet, despite its challenges, New River remains a link to the past, a path to the future, to be treasured and enjoyed.

AUTHOR'S COMMENTS

After reading the manuscript for this book in advance of its publication, historian Rodney Dillion commented that I had packed a lot of information into a relatively short book. That was my intention—to piece together much that has been written over decades into one compact, easy-to-read story of Fort Lauderdale's New River and to include some of the key figures and events from the area's history. My hope is that the casual reader will come away with a greater appreciation of New River, the aboriginal Natives who first lived on its shores, the pioneer settlers from places near and far, and the dramatic changes that came to the area beginning in the late 1800s. I also hope that this book sparks a desire for more information—much of which can be found in the excellent material listed in the bibliography.

Because there was so much to say, I tried to keep the stories—tempting as they may be—from drifting too far away from New River. In doing so, I confess that some of the storylines remain unfinished and that some of the important details were omitted. For the curious, this book should be a beginning.

In trying to understand and explain the stories of the Natives who first inhabited Florida, I admit that I glossed over important details. For example, I have given little attention to the Miccosukees, who, today, share the Everglades with the Seminoles. To learn more, I suggest that the books by Joe Knetsch and James Covington are good starting places.

There appears to be a discrepancy in the day of the week the Cooley family was killed. Dr. Cooper Kirk's incredible article in *Broward Legacy* said that the attack happened on Monday, January 6, 1836. However, online sources state that January 6 of that year was a Wednesday. For consistency's sake, I left the days of that horrible week the way they were written by Dr. Kirk.

The present locations of the Florida Historical Markers for the first and second military forts named for Major William Lauderdale differ from the descriptions from various sources used herein. The marker for the first fort is located at 400 Southwest 11th Avenue, the second at 630 Southwest 9th Avenue. The marker for the third Fort Lauderdale is located on a wall at the beach across from today's Bahia Mar.

The complex financial relationships of the Florida Coast Line Canal and Transportation Company and its tangled connections with Henry Flagler and other financiers are omitted from this book, but they are meticulously explained in Bill Crawford's *Florida's Big Dig*.

Legends and Lore of Florida's Ancient New River is roughly arranged chronologically; however, some storylines required me to travel backward or forward in time. Also, portions of some storylines are repeated elsewhere to provide context. Like a river, history often meanders.

NOTES

Chapter 1

1. "The Wonderful Legend of New River," *Fort Lauderdale Sentinel*, February 18, 1921, 6.
2. Ibid.
3. "On the Banks of the Beautiful Himmarshee" and "The Soul of Himmarshee," *Fort Lauderdale Sentinel*, February 18, 1921, 4–5.
4. Covington, *Seminoles*, 3.
5. Raymond, "Legend of New River," 7.
6. Oishimaya Sen Nag, "Largest Lakes in the U.S.," www.worldatlas.com.
7. Mizelle, "Everglades," 9.
8. Raymond, "Legend of New River," 5.
9. Lloyd, Bond and Ramdeen, "Rocks and Minerals," 1.
10. Sowers, "Failures in Limestone," 771–74.
11. Kleinberg, "Sinkholes and Earthquakes?"
12. Lane, "Earthquakes," 8–9.
13. "Florida Keys and Cuba Rattled by Rare Quake," *Miami Herald*, January 9, 2014.
14. NBC Miami, www.NBCMiami.com.
15. Kirk, "Foundations," 4.
16. Kersey, *Stranahans*, 2.
17. Ibid.
18. Gore, "Reminiscences," 3.

19. Milanich, *Florida's Indians*, 123.
20. Kersey, *Stranahans*, 2–3.
21. Gore, "Reminiscences," 4.

Chapter 2

22. Milanich, *Florida's Indians*, vii.
23. Ibid.
24. McGoun, *Ancient Miamians*, 47.
25. National Park Service, www.nps.gov.
26. Douglas, *Everglades*, 53.
27. Ibid., 54.
28. Gannon, *New History*, 16.
29. Ibid.
30. Ibid., 19.
31. Milanich, *Florida's Indians*, viii.
32. Douglas, *Everglades*, 149.
33. Ibid., 152.
34. Milanich, *Florida's Indians*, 178.
35. Seminole Tribe of Florida, "Green Corn Dance," www.semtribe.com.
36. John K. Mahon and Brent R. Weisman, "Florida's Seminoles and Miccosukee Peoples," in *The New History of Florida* (Gainesville: University Press of Florida, 1996), 189.
37. Ibid., 185–89.
38. Florida Museum, "Fort Mose," www.floridamuseum.ufl.edu.
39. Mahon and Weisman, "Seminoles and Miccosukee," 193.
40. Federal Writers' Project, *Florida*, 42.
41. White, "Military Strategy," 13.
42. Williams, *Territory*, 61.
43. White, "Military Strategy," 10.
44. Florida Department of State, "Seminole Wars."
45. Mahon and Weisman, "Seminoles and Miccosukee Peoples," 198.

Chapter 3

46. McIver, *Touched*, 130.
47. Ibid., 131.

48. Murdoch, "Documents Concerning a Voyage," 33.
49. Kirk, "Broward's Legend," 12.
50. Scott, "The Many Heirs of Jonathan Lewis," 3.
51. Ibid., 4.
52. Douglas, *Everglades*, 33.
53. Motte, *Journey into Wilderness*, 222.
54. Kirk, "Broward's Legend, Part 1," 14.
55. Ibid.
56. Ibid., 15.
57. Ibid., 16.
58. Ibid.

Chapter 4

59. A photograph of Colee Massacre plaque from the Fort Lauderdale Historical Society Research Library.
60. City of Fort Lauderdale Proclamation dated January 3, 1934.
61. "Colee Massacre Monument to Be Dedicated Next Week," *Fort Lauderdale News*, March 10, 1934, 1.
62. "Monument Is Erected in Fort Lauderdale Where Members of Colee Family Died," family papers of Ethel Colee, Broward County Historical Archives, Broward County Library.
63. Miner, *Broward County*, 3; Douglas, *Everglades*, 174–75; Hanna and Hanna, *Golden Sands*, 113.
64. George Colee christening record dated July 26, 1801.
65. Sastre, "Picolata on the St. Johns," 181.
66. Stout, "Colee Legend Mostly Myth," *Fort Lauderdale News,* July 11, 1954.
67. McGoun, "New Facts Challenge Story of Local Massacre," *Miami Herald*, November 25, 1973.
68. Dillon, "Early Broward," 39.

Chapter 5

69. Kirk, "Broward's Legend, Part 1," 17.
70. Ibid.
71. Douglas, *Everglades*, 163.
72. Ibid., 162.

73. Kirk, "Broward's Legend, Part 1," 17.
74. Ibid., 18.
75. Weildling and Burghard, *Checkered Sunshine*, 4.
76. Kirk, "Broward's Legend, Part 1," 18.
77. Kirk, "Broward's Legend, Part 2," 24, 27.
78. Knetsch, "Land Office," 21.
79. Kirk, "Broward's Legend," 18.

Chapter 6

80. Davidson, "Last Campaign."
81. Historical Society of Palm Beach County, www.hspbc.org.
82. Davidson, "Last Campaign."
83. Weidling and Burghard, *Checkered Sunshine*, 5.
84. Ibid., 6.
85. Ibid., 7.
86. Gore, "Reminiscences," 4.
87. Dillon, "Early Broward," 42.

Chapter 7

88. Knetsch, "Second Ending," 23.
89. Ibid., 24.
90. Knetsch, *Seminole Wars*, 150.
91. Staubach, "Civil War," *Tequesta*, 36.
92. Shofner and Gannon, ed., *The New History of Florida*, 249.
93. Gannon, *Florida*, 48.
94. Eck, "Ending the Hunt," 24.
95. Landini, "Keepers," 18.
96. Ibid., 20.

Chapter 8

97. Henshall, *Camping and Cruising*, 2.
98. Kirk, "Foundations," 7.
99. Ibid., 6.

100. Henshall, *Camping and Cruising*, 233.
101. Brickell, *William and Mary Brickell*, 45.
102. Britannica Online Encyclopedia, www.britannica.com.
103. Brickell, *William and Mary Brickell*, 49.
104. McIver, "Stagecoach."
105. "Stagecoach," *Broward Legacy*, 37–42.
106. Kersey, *Stranahans*, 68.
107. Ibid., 47–49.
108. Crawford, *Florida's Big Dig*, 10.
109. Ibid., 12.
110. Ibid., 10.
111. Kersey, *Stranahans*, 29.
112. Kirk, "Foundations," 7.
113. Crawford, *Florida's Big Dig*, 66.
114. Graham, *Mr. Flagler's St. Augustine*, 33–34.
115. Ibid., 41.
116. Graham, *Awakening*, 166.
117. Martin, *Flagler: Visionary*, 89–90.
118. Graham, *Mr. Flagler's St. Augustine*, 149.
119. Bramson, *Speedway to Sunshine*, 56.
120. Brickell, *William and Mary Brickell*, 70.
121. Chandler, *Henry Flagler*, 169.
122. Ibid.
123. Gillis, *Venice of America*, 18.
124. Ibid., 20.
125. Model Land Company records, University of Miami Special Collections, ASM0075.
126. Bramson, *Speedway to Sunshine*, 67.
127. Weilding and Burghard, *Checkered Sunshine*, 21.
128. Kersey, *Stranahans*, 146–48.

Chapter 9

129. Douglas, *Everglades*, 202–3.
130. Mahon and Weisman, "Seminoles and Miccosukee Peoples," 201.
131. Douglas, *Everglades*, 215.
132. Crawford, *Florida's Big Dig*, 9.
133. Ibid., 9.

134. Kirk, "Foundations," 3.

135. Proctor, *Napoleon*, 35.

136. Ibid., 18.

137. Ibid., 23–32.

138. Ibid., 41, 53–54.

139. Ibid., 78.

140. Kirk, "Foundations," 7.

141. Proctor, *Napoleon*, 190–91.

142. Ibid., 192.

143. Kirk, "Foundations," 8.

144. Ibid.

145. Inscription on the back of postcard "Surveyors in the Everglades," circa 1911.

146. Weidling and Burghard, *Checkered Sunshine*, 29.

147. Ibid., 41.

148. Proctor, *Napoleon*, 305, 308, 310.

149. Weidling and Burghard, *Checkered Sunshine*, 43.

150. Kirk, "Foundations," 10.

151. Ibid., 11.

152. Courtesy of Rodney Dillon and Barbara Poleo, Past Perfect Florida History, History Fort Lauderdale.

153. Kirk, "Foundations," 7.

154. Deed number 14457, recorded on August 4, 1891, Broward County Library Archives.

155. "Memories, Surveying South Florida in the 1870s," *Broward Legacy* 9, no. 1 (1986): 6.

156. Kersey, *Stranahans*, 98.

157. Port Everglades History, www.porteverglades.net.

Chapter 10

158. Kirk, "Broward's Legend," 14.

159. Raymond, "Legend of New River," 4.

160. Author's 2020 interview with Phil Purcell, the chief executive officer of Marine Industries Association of South Florida.

161. Port Everglades History.

162. *South Florida Sun-Sentinel*, June 13, 2020.

BIBLIOGRAPHY

Anonymous. "An Historic Site," *New River News* 17, no. 3 (1979).
———. "Monuments and Markers." *New River News* 3, no. 3 (n.d.).
———. "Stone Will Recall Massacre by Indians." Colee family files, St. Augustine Historical Society Research Library.
Barnes, Jay. *Florida's Hurricane History*. Chapel Hill: University of North Carolina Press, 1998.
Bramson, Seth H. *Broward County*. Charleston, SC: Arcadia Publishing, 2017.
———. *Speedway to Sunshine: The Story of the Florida East Coast Railway*. Ontario, CA: Boston Mills Press, 2010.
Brickell, Beth. *William and Mary Brickell: Founders of Miami & Fort Lauderdale*. Charleston, SC: The History Press, 2011.
Brooks, James Thomas, Jr. "Napoleon Broward and the Great Land Debate." *Broward Legacy* 11, no. 1–2 (Winter/Spring 1988): 41–44.
Cash, William Thomas. *The Story of Florida*. New York: American Historical Society, 1938.
Chandler, David Leon. *Henry Flagler: The Astonishing Life and Times of the Visionary Robber Baron Who Founded Florida*. New York: MacMillan Publishing Company, 1986.
Cohen, M.M. *Notices of Florida and the Campaigns*. Charleston, SC: 1838. Facsimile of the first edition. Gainesville: University of Florida Press, 1960.
Colee, Samuel J. "George Colee—His Record." Colee family files, St. Augustine Historical Society Research Library.
Covington, James W. *The Seminoles of Florida*. Gainesville: University Press of Florida, 1993.

Crawford, William G., Jr. *Florida's Big Dig: The Atlantic Intracoastal Waterway from Jacksonville to Miami 1881 to 1935*. Cocoa: Florida Historical Society Press, 2006.

————. "A History of Florida's East Coast Canal." *Broward Legacy* 20, nos. 3–4 (Summer/Fall 1997): 2–28.

Davidson, Bob. "The Last Campaign of Major William Lauderdale: 1838." *Origins and History of the Palm Beaches, The Last Campaign of Major William Lauderdale*. www.pbchistory.blogspot.com.

Dillon, Rodney E., Jr. "Legends of Early Broward." *Broward Legacy* 10, nos. 1–2 (1987): 37–45.

Douglas, Marjory Stoneman. *The Everglades: River of Grass*. New York: Reinhart & Company, 1947.

Eck, Christopher R. "Ending the Hunt for 'Pig' Brown." *Broward Legacy* 29, no. 1 (2009): 22–36.

Fass, Herbert I. "The History of the St. Augustine Transfer Company." *Carriage Journal*, n.d.

Federal Writers' Project of the Work Projects Administration for the State of Florida. *Florida: A Guide to the Southernmost State*. New York: Oxford University Press, 1939.

Florida Department of State. "The Seminole Wars." www.myflorida.com.

Gaines, Jim. "Fort Nowhere." *Broward–Palm Beach New Times*, April 25, 2002.

Gannon, Michael. *Florida, A Short History*. Gainesville: University Press of Florida, 2003.

Gannon, Michael, ed. *The New History of Florida*. Gainesville: University Press of Florida, 1996.

Gillis, Susan. *Fort Lauderdale: The Venice of America*. Charleston, SC: Arcadia Publishing, 2004.

Gore, Robert H., III. "Reminiscences of a River." *Broward Legacy* 19, nos. 1–2 (1996): 2–18.

Graham, Thomas. *The Awakening of St. Augustine*. St. Augustine, FL: St. Augustine Historical Society, 1978.

Hanna, Alfred Jackson, and Kathryn Abbey Hanna. *Florida's Golden Sands*. New York: Bobbs-Merrill Company Inc., 1950.

Henshall, James A., MD. *Camping and Cruising in Florida*. Cincinnati, OH: Robert Clark & Co., 1884. www.amazon.com.

Historical Society of Palm Beach County. "Early Tribes: Seminoles and Miccosukees," www.palmbeachhistoryonline.org.

————. "Early Tribes: Tequesta." www.pbchistoryonline.org.

———. "The 2nd Seminole War in Palm Beach County." www. pbchistoryonline.org.

Jupiter: Florida Inland Navigation District. "History of F.I.N.D." www.aicw.org.

Kersey, Harry. *The Stranahans of Fort Lauderdale*. Gainesville: University of Florida Press, 2003.

Kirk, Cooper. "The Abortive Attempt to Create Broward County in 1913." *Broward Legacy* 12, nos. 1–2 (1989): 2–27.

———. "The Failure to Create Broward County: 1913." *Broward Legacy* 11, no. 3 (1988): 2–4.

———. "Foundations of Broward County Waterways." *Broward Legacy* 8, nos. 1–2 (1985): 2–19.

———. "William Cooley: Broward's Legend, Part One." *Broward Legacy* 1, no. 1 (1976): 12–20.

———. "William Cooley: Broward's Legend, Part Two." Fort Lauderdale: *Broward Legacy* 1, no. 2 (1977): 24–36.

Kleinberg, Eliot. "Does Florida Get Sinkholes and Earthquakes?" *Palm Beach Post*, April 2, 2020.

Knetsch, Joe. *Florida's Seminole Wars 1817–1858*. Charleston, SC: Arcadia Publishing, 2003.

———. "Not Everyone Liked the Brickells." *South Florida History* 28, no. 2 (Spring 2000): 10–15.

———. "A Second Ending: Broward in the Indian Scare of 1849." *Broward Legacy* 11, no. 3 (1988): 22–24.

———. "William Cooley and the Land Office." *Broward Legacy* 16, no. 1 (1993): 21–24.

———. "William Cooley Explores the Everglades." *Broward Legacy* 12, no. 1–2 (1989): 40–44.

Landini, Ruth. "Keepers of Fort Lauderdale's House of Refuge." *Broward Legacy* 31, no. 1 (2011): 18–26.

Lane, Ed. "Earthquakes and Seismic History of Florida." *Florida Geological Survey*, February 1991.

Lloyd, J.M., P.A. Bond and S.E. Ramdeen. "Florida's Rocks and Minerals." *Florida Geological Survey*, 2009.

Martin, Sidney Walter. *Henry Flagler: Visionary of the Gilded Age*. Lake Buena Vista, FL: Tailored Tours Publications, 1998.

McGoun, William E. *Ancient Miamians: The Tequesta of South Florida*. Gainesville: University Press of Florida, 2002.

———. "New Facts Change Story of Local Massacre." *Miami Herald*, November 25, 1973.

McIver, Stuart. "Stagecoach to Miami." *Sun-Sentinel*, June 4, 1989.
———. *Touched by the Sun*. Sarasota, FL: Pineapple Press, 2001.

Menga, Ralph J., and Patrick R. Currie. "Draining the Everglades." *Broward Legacy* 2, no. 3 (1978): 29–33.

Milanich, Jerald T. *Florida's Indians from Ancient Times to the Present*. Gainesville: University Press of Florida, 1998.

Miner, Frances H. *History of Broward County*. Federal Writers' Project American Guide Series. Miami: Work Projects Administration for the State of Florida, July 15, 1936.

Mizelle, John B. "Florida's Everglades." *Weekly Miami Metropolis*, January 30, 1903.

Motte, Jacob Rhett, and James F. Sunderman, ed. *Journey into Wilderness*. Gainesville: University of Florida Press, 1963.

Murdoch, Richard K. "Documents Concerning a Voyage to the Miami Region in 1793." *Broward Legacy* 3, nos. 3–4 (1979): 32–37.

Patterson, Marjorie D. "The Old Forts." *New River News* 15, no. 4 (April 30, 1977).

Pierce, Charles W., and Donald Walter Curl, ed. *Pioneer Life in Southeast Florida*. Coral Gables, FL: University of Miami Press, 1970.

Proctor, Samuel. *Napoleon Bonaparte Broward*. Gainesville: University of Florida Press, 1950.

Raymond, Bill. "The Legend of New River—Fact or Fiction?" *New River News* 22, no. 4 (Spring 1984): 1–8.

Reprinted from *Fort Lauderdale Herald*. "Facts about Fort Lauderdale and Broward County." *Broward Legacy* 9, nos. 3–4 (1986): 42–44.

Rose, R.E. *The Swamp and Overflow Lands of Florida*. Tallahassee: Florida State College for Women, 1916.

Sastre, Cicile-Marie. "Picolata on the St. Johns: St. Augustine's River Outpost." Dissertation, Florida State University College of Arts and Sciences, 1998. St. Augustine Historical Society Research Library.

Schmidt, Bruno. "Colee Hammock." Colee family files, St. Augustine Historical Society Research Library, November 16, 1958.

Scott, Patrick S. "The Many Heirs of Jonathan Lewis." *Broward Legacy* 17, nos. 3–4 (1994): 2–23.

Scott, Patrick S., ed. "The Hunt in Florida: The Senie Douthit Letter." *Broward Legacy* 21, nos. 1–2 (1998): 2–17.

Sowers, George F. "Failures in Limestone in Humid Subtropics." *Journal of the Geotechnical Engineering Division* 101, no. GT8 (August 1975).

Staubach, Col. James C. "Miami During the Civil War, 1861–65." Miami: *Tequesta*, no. 53 (1953): 31–62.

St. Augustine Record. "Sands of Time—50 Years Ago." March 16, 1984.

———. "St. Johns and St. Augustine Canal Company." December 22, 1838.

Stout, Wesley W. "The Beachcomber." *Fort Lauderdale News,* July 11, 12 and 13, 1954; January 22, 1960; February 28 and 29, 1960; March 1 and 9, 1960; November 22, 1960.

Taylor, Robert A. "Unforgotten Threat: Florida Seminoles in the Civil War." *Florida Historical Quarterly* 69, no. 3 (1991): 300–14.

Titusville Advocate, reprinted in *Tropical Sun* (Juno), March 9, 1893. "Stagecoach Visits Fort Lauderdale in 1893." *Broward Legacy* 9, nos. 1–2 (1986): 37–42.

Wallace, John. *Carpet-Bag Rule in Florida: The Inside Workings.* Jacksonville, FL: D.A. Costa Printing and Publishing House, 1888. Facsimile reproduction of first edition. Gainesville: University of Florida Digital Collections, 1964.

Weidling, Philip. "Port Everglades at Bay Mabel." *New River News* 16, no. 4 (1978).

Weidling, Philip, and August Burghard. *Checkered Sunshine.* Fort Lauderdale, FL: Fort Lauderdale Historical Society, 1974. Revised edition under arrangement with the Fort Lauderdale Historical Society. Fort Lauderdale: Wake-Brook House, n.d.

White, John C., Jr. "American Military Strategy During the Second Seminole War." Master's thesis, Marine Corps Command and Staff College, April 1995. www.globalsecurity.org.

Wiley, Eugene E. "Life Saving Station #4." *Broward Legacy* 1, no. 1 (1976): 36–39.

Williams, Arthur T. "Memories: Surveying South Florida in the 1870s." *Broward Legacy* 9, no. 1 (1986): 2–10.

Williams, John Lee. *The Territory of Florida.* First published, New York: A.T. Goodrich, 1837. Gainesville: University of Florida Press, 1962. Carlisle, MA: Applewood Books, 2016.

INDEX

N

Native tribes
  Apalachees 19
  Calusas 19
  Creek 19, 30, 39, 57, 58
  Miccosukee 37
  Seminoles 19, 24, 30, 31, 32, 33, 34, 36, 37, 46, 57, 64, 65, 69, 71
  Tequesta 9, 10, 19, 24, 26, 39, 129
  Timucuans 19
New River Inlet 24, 41, 75, 79, 125
New River Sound 41, 73, 91, 92, 105, 118
North New River Canal 18, 116, 130

O

orange blossoms 97
Ormand, Hotel 96
Osceola 34, 57, 64, 65

P

Palm Beach 24, 26, 49, 96, 99, 118, 120, 130
Parrott, Joseph R. 97
Pay-hai-okee 25, 30, 37
Pine Island 65, 80
Pompano 120
Ponce de Leon, Hotel 96
Ponce de Leon, Juan 26, 29, 30
Proctor, Samuel 108
Pynchon, E.A. 50

Q

Quesada, Juan Nepomuceno de 40, 42

R

Raymond, Bill 19, 20
Reconstruction era 72, 110
Rigby, Mary R. 55
Rockefeller, John D. 82

S

Scott, Patrick S. 43
Seminoles. *See* Native tribes
Seminoles, Black 32
Seminole Wars 32, 34, 36, 37, 56, 57, 64, 70, 80, 106
Shofner, Jerrell H. 72
Shourds, Ida Alice. *See* Flagler, Ida Alice
Smith, Buckingham 105, 107
Spain ceded Florida to the United States 32
Standard Oil 82
Staubach, James C. 71
St. Augustine 10, 30, 31, 41, 50, 52, 53, 54, 55, 75, 82, 89, 94, 95, 99
St. Augustine Historical Society 50
St. Augustine Transfer Company 89
stickball 31
Stout, Wesley W. 53
Stranahan, Frank 85, 86, 87, 92, 104

ABOUT THE AUTHOR

Donn R. Colee Jr. is a seventh-generation Floridian and a direct descendant of George Colee, who immigrated to the St. Augustine area from England in 1821. Donn grew up in Orlando but frequently visited relatives in the ancient city, where his curiosity was piqued by stories about a massacre of long-ago family members at Fort Lauderdale's New River. While the "Colee Massacre" story was later debunked, it refused to die. His book began as an attempt to finally resolve the last vestiges of that myth, but the power of New River quickly propelled the book to become a history of the river, its fascinating people, and the transformation of its wilderness into a metropolis. Colee is a member of the Florida Historical Society, Fort Lauderdale Historical Society, St. Augustine Historical Society, and Historical Society of Palm Beach County. He is a former commissioner of the Florida Inland Navigation District, the state agency responsible for maintenance and improvements of the Atlantic Intracoastal Waterway from Fernandina Beach to Key Biscayne. It was built by a company that was cofounded in 1881 by his great-great-great-grandfather, who became its civil engineer.

This is Colee's second book. His first, *Towers in the Sand*, is a history of the broadcasting industry in Florida, a business his family has been engaged in for three generations. Today, he resides in Palm Beach Gardens.

Visit us at
www.historypress.com